The Past Isn't Over

So, you're feeling stuck. Something has got a hold on you and won't let go. It's your Past and it isn't going away. You can't get away from it until you confront it. Yes, the boogieman won't bother you anymore, once you get the courage to look under the bed.

Healing the Past gives you the courage to look under that bed and right into your past from this lifetime and many other lifetimes. You'll be surprised at how long the bad old boogieman (your fears, insecurities, and self-defeating behaviors) has been stalking you.

Author Arian Sarris gives you a totally new perspective that is informative and healing on both a psychological and a spiritual level. More importantly, she gives you the tools to slay your inner monsters from the past and reemerge into the present through a transformative spiritual opening.

You will learn how to access your Higher Self or inner wisdom, Guardian Angel, and a host of heavenly helpers. This book shows you what kinds of blocks are in the way to your personal growth, and how to get rid of them once and for all. Moreover, you'll find out how to align yourself with your life or soul purpose through powerful guided exercises. Free yourself from the past and step forward into your future.

About the Author

Arian Sarris is a licensed transpersonal Marriage, Family, and Child Counselor, and a practicing psychic and conscious channeler. As a psychotherapist, she guides clients in experiencing change. She has taught psychic and channeling classes, hypnotherapy, couple counseling, spiritual healing, pre-natal bonding, self-growth, etc. She has written and had published a number of short stories and articles, both in the United States and in Europe. Arian currently practices in Oregon, teaching many of the above subjects.

Tapes are available for many of the exercises used in this book. Please write to the author for information.

To Write to the Author

If you wish to contact the author or would like more information about this book, please write to the author in care of Llewellyn Worldwide, and we will forward your request. Both the author and publisher appreciate hearing from you and learning of your enjoyment of this book and how it has helped you. Llewellyn Worldwide cannot guarantee that every letter written to the author can be answered, but all will be forwarded. Please write to:

Llewellyn's New Worlds of Mind and Spirit
P.O. Box 64383–K601–7, St. Paul, MN 55164-0383,
U.S.A.
Please enclose a self-addressed, stamped envelope for reply,
or $1.00 to cover costs.
If outside the U.S.A., enclose international postal reply coupon.

GETTING ON WITH YOUR LIFE ...

HEALING THE PAST

ARIAN SARRIS

1997
Llewellyn Publications
St. Paul, Minnesota, U.S.A. 55164-0383

FIRST EDITION, 1997
First Printing

Cover design by Anne Marie Garrison
Cover photo: Cowgirl Stock Photography
Interior design and editing by Connie Hill

Library of Congress Cataloging-in-Publication Data
Sarris, Arian, 1946–
    Healing the past : getting on with your life... / Arian
Sarris — 1st ed.
      p.   cm. —)
Includes bibliographical references.
    ISBN 1-56718-601–7 (trade pbk.)
    1. Change (Psychology). 2. Mind and body.
3. Spiritual Life. 4. New Age movement. I. Title.
BF637.C4S27   1997
131—dc20   97-949
                                           CIP

Llewellyn Publications
A Division of Llewellyn Worldwide, Ltd.
St. Paul, Minnesota 55164-0383, U.S.A.

ACKNOWLEDGEMENTS

To Intz Walker, who believed in me,
even when I despaired
(we all deserve a friend like that).

To Leya Steele, whose insights contributed
to many of my understandings.

And to those noisy seagulls out at Ocean Beach,
who came along with me to heal the past.

TABLE OF CONTENTS

LAYERS OF THE PAST

We are shaped by our childhood environment—the family situation, the abuse and dysfunction, and the beliefs we create accordingly to survive. The purpose for writing *Healing the Past* was to show how to break free of the constraints that the past puts on you by confronting those issues, patterns, programs, and fears, and finding ways to counteract their effects.

Besides your childhood, another layer of the past that controls you is your past lives. Think of those core problems that you struggled with for years. Even though you might find some relief and release through therapy, it still persists. As I have guided clients to work at deeper levels, they often spontaneously go into past life situations, where we can resolve them at a soul level.

What is remarkable about past life work is that you can process as powerfully as if you are remembering your present-day childhood, and more importantly, you can begin to discover solutions to other intractable problems, such as phobias, allergies, and disease. By using the techniques in this book, you will make serious strides toward breaking free of your controlling patterns—if you choose—and at your own pace.

In this book you will find suggestions for dealing with specific situations and issues:

- Find ways to break free of the constraints of the past—both in your current and past lives.

- Discover your own solutions to phobias, allergies, and self-complexes.

- Use tools and exercises to create change and movement in your life—visualization, past life work, metaphor, guides, and Higher Self.

- Move away from the victim/blame roles.

- Begin to understand karmic issues as they manifest in your life, and take responsibility for changing them—in past lives and now.

- Understand the larger purpose of disease, and work on freeing it from your life.

- Explore your life purpose and set yourself on track toward reaching your inner goals.

You will discover the five parts of which we are made: mind, body, emotions, aura, and soul. You can use and experience tools (psychic and psychological) and resources (such as angels and the Higher Self) that will become necessary helpers. You will look at a full spectrum of issues around your present life—the mind and self-image, the emotions (Inner Child) and child-hood abuse, reversal of energy, who you attract and why, pivotal moments in your life, your lifestream process, and past life work—including karma, phobias, disease, core issues and life purpose. In these chapters you will find exercises to help you work through your issues.

Many psychotherapy books address the patterns of childhood and ways to break them that cut across the whole spectrum of approaches (Freudian, Jungian, humanistic, existential, traditional, transpersonal, etc.), but that's where these books stop. By employing non-traditional psychological, spiritual, and psychic techniques, I have provided tools to help you create movement in your life. You will use metaphysics, spiritual concepts, and psychic techniques such as visualization, past life work, metaphor, guides, and the Higher Self to heal your past and help you move forward into your future.

We have been called a nation of victims. When we feel helpless and overwhelmed by our patterns, it is hard to find a way out except by blaming others. *Healing the Past* gives you another option for breaking through your internal log jam of blame to reach self-acceptance, and, ultimately, forgiveness of yourself and others.

By using the techniques, you will learn here in your ongoing process of transformation, you will be able to release the baggage you have been holding onto for life-times. Isn't it time to stop being controlled by your past, and open to the possibility and joy of the present?

CHAPTER 1

CHANGE YOUR LIFE

Are you ready to change your life? To get out of the rut you've been stuck in? To break out of the old way of thinking, acting, and believing?

Ask yourself the following questions: Does your life work? Are you happy? Have you forgiven your parents for your childhood? Or are you stuck in memories of those days—the abuse, the anger, the helplessness, the abandonment? Do you want to let go of the past, or do you want to still be controlled by it?

The answers to these very important questions will affect how ready you are for deep inner change. The purpose of *Healing the Past* is to help you break free of those compulsions and urges that keep you locked into old patterns of behavior and belief, not only so that you can make new choices, but so that you can step forward into your life purpose.

What is inside you that pushes you to change? That is a question I have wrestled with for many years.

After all, how flawed are we? Or how perfect? We all have our own concept of what perfection is, based, of course, on our family backgrounds, but we all agree on one thing—we aren't perfect. Actually, I'd like to let you in on a little secret: *None* of us is perfect, no matter how much our parents and other people try to convince you and me that they are. Unless they're Jesus or Buddha, perfected beings just don't exist on this planet.

If we're not perfect, and the chances of becoming perfect are seemingly as remote as virgin birth, where does that leave us? Maybe it's important to rethink the word "perfect." Some people say that everything, including us, is perfect at every moment. Their point is that it's useless to strive to reach an amorphous, unrealistic perfection which can only make us feel more imperfect. We should focus on where we are at all times.

I define "perfection" as the movement toward expressing your life purpose; therefore, whatever you do that moves you in that direction is perfection. That takes perfection out of the hands of others and puts it smack where it belongs—inside you. Only you can know your direction and how to move forward. You might actually wake up one morning and decide that you're now ready to accept yourself as you are, and that you are perfectly on your path, no matter how long it takes.

I believe that within each of us there is an inexorable movement toward manifesting our life purpose, the purpose we came onto this planet to fulfill. Sometimes we discover it early in life, but most of us find it in our late thirties and forties, after we've been working to clear away many of our inner blocks. When you manifest your life purpose, it feels like everything has fallen into place; and conversely, when you are not fulfilling it, you feel discontented, frustrated, and unhappy.

Your soul wants you to function at your maximum capability. A 100 percent commitment to your work (whether it is your external job or internal evolution) may be difficult because a major part of your energy is locked away in old patterns, beliefs, fears, and addictions.

The extent to which you are governed by these experiences and fears indicates the level of control the past has over you—in how you think, act, and respond to the world. It's hard to have faith that the future will be anything different—and yet it can be. Your conditioning has managed to shackle your mind and body and created a seemingly unalterable present and future by shutting you off from your own divinity and your own greater wisdom and love.

You are not here to suffer needlessly (as many of us think), but rather to break free of old, destructive belief systems, and embrace love and joy. For your own growth, you need to free up this energy. Given a chance, you can do just that—by transforming the past.

Every time you trigger a memory, you release trapped energy at every level of your being. It's like cleaning out an abscess. First you feel a sharp pain, as the emotion (for instance: anger or sadness) pours out of you; then you feel a wonderful sensation of relief as the abscess is finally cleansed of its toxins (the memory is transformed). Each time that happens, profound changes ripple throughout all levels of your being—from your heart and mind to your physical body and

even your soul. Your triumphs over your past conditioning can be measured in the gains you perceive in your
self-wisdom, self-love, and the practice and manifestation of your higher purpose.

With each memory that you clear, space opens
inside you for something else to flow into you, something you may not believe you deserve—healing joy
and love. At first, those energies may need to be provided by higher beings like angels—then, as you become
more comfortable basking in that feeling of love, by
your Higher Self, and ultimately, you.

Changing the past works by releasing the root cause
of your unwanted or outworn behavior; but how can
you change what has already happened? After all, the
past is the *past*. It is impossible to go back and reshape
it without using a time machine. That is true—in one
sense. If your father beat you when you were a child,
you can't change that reality. But—and this is a big
but—you can change its impact inside of you.

In order for change to occur, you need a safe environment—surroundings that encourage you to grow at
your own speed and as you feel comfortable, without
criticism, judgment, or pressure. This is extremely important. Being browbeaten to make changes may force
some level of transformation, but when it is accomplished in fear and unhappiness, it causes more misery
and prevents love and joy from being part of your transformative process. You've had enough of that. Instead, I
invite you to experience change in love and joy.

The process of healing starts with childhood issues
because not only is it the easiest time period to access, it

4

usually has the greatest "juice." Your childhood survival depended on fitting in with your family structure, by cultivating those behaviors that were acceptable in your environment, and eliminating the ones that might leave you unloved, abandoned, or hurt, either emotionally or physically. That may have meant submitting to awful abuse because there was simply no other way of getting nurturing or of staying alive.

As a child, after undergoing abuse or trauma, you unintentionally disconnected yourself from your Higher Self, and closed down critical parts of yourself (whether it was your heart, your mind, or your intuition). Doing so took so much of your life force that you had only enough energy left to focus on getting your survival needs met. Being yourself was not acceptable.

Now that you have grown up, the pain from those childhood traumas and needs still remains embedded in your emotional body (see Chapters 2 and 8), quiescent until some event triggers it, like marrying an abusive, clingy, alcoholic, or neglectful spouse. It is always there—waiting. When the traumas get activated, the same fear you experienced as a child rushes back, as potent now as it was then—and you react in the same way. Gone are any adult behaviors and resources; you have been caught by the situation. You may even regress and act like a child, especially when the memory is severe, such as suddenly recovered sexual abuse memories.

To demonstrate, imagine one of the most stressful situations you can have—visiting your family. There can be nothing more intense than dealing with your parents, even for a short time. It is a rare person who can remain an adult (no matter how old you are) under the onslaught of parental attitudes and childhood conditioning or fears. You fall right back into your childhood behavior around them, no matter what you would prefer. Afterward, you feel angry, frustrated, and disgusted with yourself for having gotten trapped again, just like you did as a child.

The oldest part of your brain, the medulla, governs survival and the flight/fight instinct. It is always operating for your Inner Child (ages two–eleven), whether you the adult are aware of it or not. The Child never feels totally safe, and is always on alert. Every event, large or small, is judged according to your Child's need to survive, which means that he or she takes control. When you find yourself in what the Child perceives as a survival situation, the Child's survival behavior kicks in because you have stopped being an adult, and you lose any adult perspective.

Your Child's behavior helped you survive your childhood, but that's not necessarily acceptable or appropriate behavior for you now. It's time to create appropriate adult behaviors by releasing those constrictive beliefs, emotional needs, and fears. The first step is to create an alternative to those early behaviors by giving you the ability to make choices.

Your Child does not possess the psychological makeup to act with choice. That would be too dangerous. Only you, as a fully functioning adult, can do that. When you break free of your Child's fight/flight survival instinct through inner change and love, you can make decisions based on adult values and understanding, rather than childhood fears and needs. As a result, the next time you visit your parents, you will have more inner resources to call upon so you can make different choices.

Every experience in your life creates neuron pathways inside your brain and central nervous system. The more intense the emotion surrounding an event, the more hormones flood through your body, and the stronger the pathway that is created or reinforced. It's like learning a new skill—the first few times you're slow and uncoordinated, as the brain's neurons form a new pathway; but with each repetition of the skill, the path is strengthened, and you become faster and more adept.

So it is with memory. Every time you recall an event, especially one with an emotional charge, you strengthen that pathway. Altering that memory through changework (the process of meaningful, focused self-transformation) closes off that path and creates another one. As you work through your past, you can face the experience of abuse, change the memory to release the poison, and fill yourself with love.

The reconstructed memory, instead of generating the former emotional states of fear, abandonment, loss, rage, shame, etc., flows into love, forgiveness, relaxation, and peace, allowing healing to begin. This simple process removes, bit by bit, the terror and power of the past from your life. As your body readjusts and realigns to accommodate the new feelings, you raise your vibration level and take another step toward transformation.

The key to the whole process of self-transformation is love. Love does not brook hate or self-denigration. It accepts; it makes no judgment. It just is. When you are feeling traumatized, enraged, or fearful, you are contracted into a protective stance. It's very difficult to be open to change. On the other hand, healing transformation is expansive, allowing you to shed old fears, traumas, behaviors, and patterns more easily and replace them with gentle, deep healing.

It starts with forgiveness—of yourself, first, and later on, of others. If you can forgive yourself for your flaws, you begin to create a space for love to enter you. The more you forgive yourself for your attitudes, feelings, actions, and judgments, the more you can feel self-acceptance. With that acceptance comes tolerance and love, and with love, inner resistance and self-dislike drain away. If, after working through the exercises in this book, you have reached some modicum of self-acceptance, you will have created an enormous openness for your own evolution toward your life purpose.

One place to start is by forgiving yourself for not being perfect, for not doing it right, according to your parents' definition. Every time you forgive yourself, you do more to break your conditioning than all the recriminations you can heap upon yourself. (Remember, change comes with acceptance, not fear.) The first time may be difficult, but with practice, you'll be amazed at how easy it becomes to accept your flaws, and in doing so, embrace change (see Chapters 6 and 7).

At times, you may wonder whether you dare continue your self-transformation because the consequences are earthshaking. You will become an entirely different person through the process, much closer to the person envisioned by your soul.

Sometimes you may wish you could return to your previous life because it was easy and safe, no matter how dysfunctional it was. However, once you step onto the path to self-healing, it is almost impossible for you to really regress. You can try to halt your progress by making yourself sick, or having accidents, but that won't halt your growth. It will proceed anyway because your soul wants desperately to break out of its emotional and mental prisons.

I've talked about releasing the traumas of childhood. Let's take this process one step further. Many of our behaviors, patterns, and fears don't even derive from this lifetime. That means in your spiritual journey you must go back into those lives whose deeds affect you now, whether in your choice of family, childhood abuse, or the blocks that cut you off from the knowledge and love you need for your continued growth. Usually, these lifetimes have complementary or similar stories to your present lifetime—if you abused someone in a past life, she or he did the same to you in the next one, and so forth; or you may be continuing the same behavior in different lives, like being trapped in a rut.

By examining your past lives, you can stop repeating the same mistake over and over, lifetime after lifetime. When you go back and rectify those events, you begin untangling the psychic snarl of abuse between yourself and others. Moreover, as you create healing at a deep soul level, it affects not only you, but all the other people involved in that lifetime.

That is one of the payoffs of changework—changing your memories not only heals you, but it also creates healing for everyone else sharing the experience, although you may not ever know exactly the kind of healing they receive.

Change does not happen overnight. In traditional psychotherapy, talking about the problem moves the client forward inch by inch, like pulling one pebble at a time out of a wall. In changework, the pebbles come out in handfuls, so the edifice of resistance and old patterning can collapse sooner, though always under the guidance and wisdom of the Higher Self. Change also takes persistence—in the face of the unpleasant, sad, and angry feelings that arise within you and in others—and once it begins, it continues.. It's very difficult to wrench yourself off the path and fall back into the morass of old patterns and fears.

I have provided a number of changework techniques in this book that I have found to be profoundly useful strategies for change. They all involve releasing trapped energy and transforming yourself by using healing vibrations and love.

By doing changework, you open up space in your heart for a new understanding of yourself and your needs and fears, as well as forgiveness of yourself and others for their mistakes. You can accept and experience divine love and joy that will permeate your cells and affect not only this lifetime but all the others as well.

Through this self-healing process you can reclaim your lost inner power, wisdom, and self-esteem, and manifest your life purpose because you feel so fulfilled when you are doing your work.

CHAPTER 2

CHAPTER 2
THE FIVE SELVES

In order to work with your inner process, you need to understand the pieces that make up the person who is you. It starts with the soul (the immortal part of you).

Before you became embodied on earth, your soul created the conditions of your life. It designated the family it intended to join, the kind of childhood and other life experiences it wanted you to have, the karma it chose to pay back, and any lessons you needed to learn. It also gathered the resources it required for you to manifest your life purpose. After all that, the soul decided what qualities you could use to provide those life lessons, karmic paybacks, and spiritual growth. The way you manifest these qualities and resources is through your four mortal selves—the aura, physical body, mind, and emotions.

Many traditions postulate that everything on this earth can be broken down into four basic elements—earth, air, water, and fire. Those four elements do not describe the scientific structure of objects, but rather their intrinsic nature, which correlates closely with the essence of your four mortal selves.

Earth is physical, tangible, and solid—which describes your *physical body*. Air is intangible, light, and invisible—the *aura*. Water is fluid, changeable, and deep—which can be identified with your *emotions*. Fire is hot, burning, and incisive—which aptly describes your *mind*. Finally, the fifth body is the pure essence of all these other bodies combined—the soul or *Higher Self*.

When the five parts work together (as it did for those few moments when you first arrived on this earth), you have congruence. Everything is in alignment; and there is an easy flow back and forth between the soul and these other selves. You feel connected to the Godhead, continuously bathed in its tremendous love and joy, and easily able to manifest your work.

The strains of your life situation can pull you out of your inner alignment. Then you become wracked with doubts, anger, frustration, shame, and guilt, so that you get caught in the conflicting needs of the four mortal selves. It's like being behind a four-horse chariot team that is out of control—one horse pulls one way, while the rest pull another. This leads to inner conflict and turbulence, especially if one part tries to dominate the others. Good examples are the mind, which denigrates or cuts off the physical body and emotions, or the emotions, which use manipulation to remain in control.

When that split occurs, there can be no harmonious blending of energies and purpose. Instead, there is internal dissension, frustration, and stress. Some of your stresses arise in childhood; others have been embedded in the soul for lifetimes. The result is a clash and cacophony between the four elements. This internal warfare does an excellent job of keeping you fractured and unfocused, so that you cannot hear anything clearly. You forget your connection to your soul, which could and would bring you into balance—if you could even remember that it exists. You need to be restored to balance.

The surest mechanism for healing is love. Not the love most of us know—a love contaminated by needs, fears, and beliefs (your own and others)—but a transcendent, godly, expansive love that fills us with joy and delight, and makes us glad to be ourselves. This love can only shine clearly through us when we are in complete balance. This is the gold vibration—the harmonious blending of the elements inside us (see Chapter 5).

Most of us operate far below the gold level. Our blocks pull down our energy and keep us off balance. The longer they remain, the more destructive they become, not only to our energy, but to our physical body, where they manifest as disease or sickness, like cancer cells invading healthy tissue.

Since all of the bodies inhabit the same space together, and are designed to work as one unit, releasing old patterns in one body causes an energetic shift in all of them—and leads to the rebuilding of a communication that was lost over the years.

Let us examine each of the five bodies in detail.

The Etheric Body

The etheric body, or aura, is a very thick flexible sheath, invisible to the naked eye, that extends out about a foot and a half from the body. It can be seen clearly by many psychics. In its normal healthy state, it is clear and ever-shifting, like a cloud moving across the sky. This force field expands and contracts, according to your mood and situation. The soul has created your aura as a buffer for the physical body against the world.

Your aura is the most acute of your four mortal bodies because, consisting of very light energy, it can penetrate right to the truth through a person's obfuscating words and confusing emotions. Have you ever met someone and taken an instant dislike to them—a feeling later proved accurate? That is because both your aura and theirs mingled, and your aura didn't like what it sensed from the other one.

Your aura tries to communicate what it has sensed through its language of comfort/discomfort. Whenever you feel some kind of emotional reaction to someone, such as being uneasy or very happy, your aura has "spoken" to you. Unfortunately, many of us rarely pay attention to our aura's very accurate comments.

Just as your body needs cleansing when you get dirty, your aura needs cleansing as well. Since it is invisible, you are rarely aware that it picks up debris as it brushes up against other people's auras. Suppose you're sitting next to a hungry person who's obsessed with a hamburger. As your aura brushes up against his, you absorb some of his desire, and though you're neither hungry nor interested in meat, suddenly you develop an insatiable craving for a hamburger. Someone else's aura has unwittingly contaminated you.

In the past, I noticed that whenever a friend or lover got mad about something, after a while they calmed down, and then I got mad. When I finally realized that I was absorbing their anger through my aura, I immediately cleaned it off to get rid of their contaminating emotion, and set up a protective field around me.

Anyone who comes into your personal space invades your aura. You may invite people into your space (lovers, family members, friends), but often other people intrude on your space (all of the above, plus outsiders like coworkers, bosses, strangers on the street) without your permission.

The residue of their presence can intentionally linger with you, so that you may hold onto their energy for years, even lifetimes. Sometimes that energy is neutral or loving; more often it's critical, judgmental, shaming, and guilt-making.

Here's an example: when someone threatens you with a raised fist, he also takes his etheric fist and slams it into your aura. You feel the blow and flinch, even though he never physically hits you. His energy now remains in your aura as a psychic bruise until you remove it. You have held on to many emotions like these without knowing it. With such energies stuck throughout your aura, it's hard to find room for self-awareness, self-esteem, and self-love.

When you clean out your aura (see Chapter 4), you remove that unwanted alien energy. Otherwise, it remains inside you for years, affecting or blocking you in some way.

The more you tune in to your aura's sensations, the more you can trust the information that you receive. Many of us lost this faculty as children. You denied what you knew was true, and accepted what you were told by others, suppressing your own wisdom for the sake of family unity and/or personal survival. A good example is growing up with an alcoholic. Many children of alcoholics remember seeing their father drunk or passed out and being told by their mother that daddy wasn't drunk. So what do they believe—their eyes or the authority figure? This is the kind of situation that makes children think they're a little crazy and no good. They reject the truth and accept the word of the authority figure for the sake of surviving in the household. As a result of situations like that, you don't dare rely on your innate wisdom. Changework helps you to reclaim that ability.

The Physical Body

Your physical body is very dense energy called matter—denser than thought, emotions, or the aura. You can't see anything through your physical body. It exists in time and space, and it must follow the physical laws of the planet (no teleportation for it, so far). This tangible envelope of the mind, emotions, and soul is known as the human clay. When you die, your body returns to the earth (or would if we didn't embalm our bodies and lock them into incorruptible plastic caskets).

The aura creates the physical body according to the soul's instructions. Imagine the aura as a kind of fairly flexible armor or template. Inside it, the body is created, cell by cell, conforming to that template, like jewelry being cast from a mold. For example, if you are handicapped in your physical body, that is because your soul created the auric template with those qualities.

Just like your aura, your physical body collects and stores an enormous amount of energy, usually negative. As children you may have endured sexual or physical abuse. Once the physical body's bruises healed, you assumed that the trauma had vanished, but in fact it remained embedded in whatever organs were traumatized. The physical body also receives abuse through negative images thrown at it—by yourself as well as others: "Why are you so fat, why couldn't you have been taller, or your breasts bigger," etc.

> **Case Study:** Lucy* gained extra weight as a result of menopause. She'll never lose those pounds, although she has attempted for fifteen years to do just that, trying every kind of diet, pill, and exercise plan, while continually denigrating and excoriating her body for being so heavy. As a result of those negative attacks, her body has suffered one illness after another, which causes her to hate it even more.

After enough traumas accumulate in your physical body, they become so intense that your body must start

---

* All examples are composites of many clients, and names have been changed.

releasing them in some way (or die); they manifest as pain and sickness. Instead of recognizing illness for what it is—a cry for help to get rid of the emotional traumas—you look at the body as an enemy that threatens your existence. Without any kind of release, negative energies become too much for the body to bear and begin to toxify, eventually manifesting as a life-threatening disease. The most common example of this process is cancer.

For physical body healing to occur, those negative energies must be released from these now-invisible but still potent wounds. That requires a complete attitude shift and an acceptance of the body as it is—in other words, flooding it with self-esteem.

Many religions conceive of the physical body as evil, no good, worthless, and something to transcend. For eons, it was considered good form to chastise the flesh with hair shirts, fasting, flagellation, or other tortures. That attitude persists today, if not those harrowing methods. Many of you wish you could exist without being embodied. You want to be somewhere else—in your mind, in your aura, in your spirit, but not in your body.

Not surprisingly, you may tend to spend a lot of time out of your body, letting it run on automatic pilot. If you take a long drive, when you get to your destination, you may remember almost nothing you saw along the route. You zoned out—you left your body and went somewhere else.

By vacating the body, you are not aware of what's going on in or around you. When you bump into objects, that's because you're not there to guide your body. That's when you can get hurt or make unwise decisions that lead you into physical or emotional danger.

With that kind of background, it's no surprise that of all the selves, your physical body requires the most healing work and needs the most love. By acknowledging that your Higher Self chose this physical body for you, perhaps you can begin to make an effort to come into harmony with it.

The Emotional Self

A healthy emotional body allows you to stay centered, so you can handle anything that arises. Emotion is beautifully personified by the symbol of water, its movement and changeability—releasing and transmuting all the frozen energies, and rinsing away the blocks, fears, and old painful emotions, so there is room left for love, the high vibration of self-transformation, to enter.

The emotional body is centered in the heart. It is not logical, literal, or organized, but it gives you depth, empathy, and love. You experience emotions like fear, rage, abandonment, contentment, and love, from the first moment of life.

The foundation of the emotional self is love—love of self and love of others. As love fills you, you open up like a flower, while feelings like fear, sadness, and anger close you down. The best kind of love comes from within, assuring you that you are now safe and taken care of. However, if your needs are not met, you are forced to turn your focus outside of yourself, seeking people and situations that can provide them.

If I were to give a symbol for the emotional self, it would be the Inner Child, the part of us who desperately seeks emotional fulfillment. She or he governs your actions and behaviors, although much of his or her control is unconscious. Their emotional needs determine how you will interact with others—whether you will face them with openness and optimism, fear and despair, or hatred and aggression.

You can see how your past controls you most clearly in the emotional self. That's where the damage inflicted on you as a child remains trapped as trauma. If you could see your emotional self, it could appear twisted and bruised, with broken, mashed, or otherwise crippled limbs, bleeding mouth and crushed nose, damaged internal organs—a person who needs immediate emergency-room attention. That's not what you see when you look in the mirror, unless you're married to an abusive spouse. The physical envelope that holds this emotional body appears deceptively healthy. Sooner or later, however, if the emotional self's traumas are not addressed, those toxins begin to poison the physical body and create sickness—often life-threatening.

When you're caught in the grip of emotional need, you're like a teenager in puberty; your heart rules your head. A perfect example is overeating. Food has an enormous emotional significance, which most diet plans ignore. It doesn't matter how much you argue with yourself not to overeat. You can say 100 times, "I *will not* eat that chocolate ice cream. I need to lose weight, and it's not good for me." The next thing you know, the last spoonful of ice cream has disappeared down your throat. Then you chastise yourself for your lack of self-control, and hammer yourself with those judgmental phrases you know so well: "You can't do anything right; you'll always be fat; you're no good; no one will love you that way," etc.

Logic can neither sway nor argue the Child into submission, no matter how persuasive and strong the inducement, because your Child's emotional needs far outweigh your mind's arguments. If you got off the phone after a painful conversation with your lover, and you feel miserable (i.e., abandoned, unloved), eating chocolate ice cream numbs the pain a little. The Child's emotional cry for nurturance (via food) overrides your logic at the moment (but the mind gets its revenge with its continual negative mental barrage).

When your Inner Child is out of control with misery, he or she needs to feel a love so strong that it fills them completely. As he or she gets bathed in that deep love, you bathe yourself in love as well. That happens when you clear away the painful patterns that keep you locked in non-loving beliefs and behaviors. In this way you not only begin to disconnect the Inner Child from his or her fears, but you open yourself up for your own nurturance.

The Mental Self

The symbol of the mind is fire. The quality of fire is brilliant, biting, and incisive. The tarot symbolizes the mind as a sword. Consider the purpose of a sword. It's sharp, and it can shred or slice someone to ribbons. Both are excellent descriptions of the mind's faculties.

We might say that the mind is a sword because it can flay its targets unmercifully. Physical bruises heal, but the effects of ridicule and cutting words remain, destroying a person's self-esteem now and in the future.

Remember the childhood chant: "Sticks and stones will break my bones, but names will never hurt me"? Words are far more destructive than sticks and stones. I hated to be ridiculed as a child; I knew how words hurt

You think, analyze, and express yourself through your mental body. It keeps you from turning into emotional mush. The mind understands concepts, ideas, and perceptions. It extrapolates and interpolates; it's logical, it has opinions and attitudes. You can call it your ego or personality. It is also prone to rigid thinking, narrow-mindedness, "illogical logic," holding an opinion long after evidence proves that it's specious and destructive. When people say, "Stop being so emotional," they're saying, "Get back into your mental body." The mind has cachet. It is okay to hang out there, to be "rational" like Mr. Spock. Lots of logic, lots of perception—but no heart.

In its arrogance, your mind thinks it is in charge, even though it is really controlled by your childhood fears and needs. It formulates a world view according to how well you got your emotional needs met from the people and events of your early life. That means your belief system may be badly skewed, but you can't tell unless you examine it clearly and dispassionately. A fundamentalist has a rigid belief system, but a scientist can have an equally rigid one. That belief system can kill you, keep you safe, or make you happy.

What kinds of beliefs have you incorporated into your mind? Here are just two of the many that you may hold:

- The world is a dangerous place.

- You don't deserve love and you'll never be worthy of it—and you'll do everything to prove it.

Nor does your mind believe in or accept the love the Higher Self would like to give you. These are beliefs, not reality, unless you *choose* to make them real.

What if you could change any one of your beliefs? You can. Mind is certainly stronger than matter, but it takes time and energy to reprogram yourself—and the willingness to do it.

If your mind is made up, it takes a lot of words to chip away at the belief in order to alter it. That's what counseling is all about. The more flexible your mind, the more able you are to make adjustments in your beliefs. When you realize you're wrong about an idea, and your mind absorbs that lesson and adjusts, the stronger and wiser you become. With each change in your attitude, you loosen more barriers restricting your mind—whether they are self-imposed or not.

The Spiritual Body

Your immortal spiritual body is the creator of your existence on earth. I call it the *Higher Self*. Since this wise part of you resides outside the physical body (six to eight inches above your head), it has a much higher perspective of your life. It can see beyond the rigid thinking of the mental self, beyond the passion and fears of the emotional self, and beyond the pain of the physical body. Intuitions are messages from the Higher Self, or even from the Godhead.

The spiritual self is the lodestone around which you revolve—for this part of you knows exactly the right word or image to guide you forward toward your spiritual path. For that life journey, you need to align very closely with your spiritual self in order for true transformation to take place. After all, it has your well-being in mind at all times (see Chapter 3).

Love

When your body is out of balance, you cannot feel love, or you may feel it in a distorted way because it cannot come into you freely. As you heal your past and release blocks, you open a space for that love to pour into you, undiluted and unadulterated.

Even though the four mortal selves may have a difficult time experiencing love individually because of all the distractions or blocks in their way, your spiritual self holds its love and the Godhead's love in trust for you whenever you're ready to receive it. It loves you unconditionally, if you will only allow yourself to accept and feel that love.

When the four elements (earth, air, fire, and water) combine together in a balanced way, they achieve a special quality called "gold." Think of your self in the same way. When you bring the four elements or bodies into balance, they radiate a gold vibration throughout you and everyone else around you that feels wonderful, joyous, and godly.

Changework begins the process of aligning your five selves. You can clean out the different parts of your being by removing old patterns, releasing blocks, regaining lost energy, and bringing all of them into balance, so that they vibrate together in harmony (see Chapter 5). When that happens, you can once again experience the joy of connection with your Higher Self and the greater cosmic energies, and tap into your expanded potential.

• • •

CHAPTER 3

RESOURCES FOR THE JOURNEY

In any journey, particularly a spiritual one, there must be a beginning, and ours begins with the Oversoul, that immortal part of us that separated in innocence from the Godhead long aeons ago.* In its long history, the Oversoul has inhabited many different forms in every race, culture, and country as part of its quest to learn the lessons of humanity and gain the wisdom necessary to return to the Godhead. Yet the path is not easy or straightforward. It has taken twists and turns through every aspect of the human condition—and the lessons have often been painful.

In each of these lives, as we struggled toward self-understanding and wisdom, we made decisions and performed deeds which created karma (cosmic debt) that needed to be paid off, in that lifetime or in later

---

* In all the changework that is described in this book, I will be calling on the assistance of many kinds of beings. If you have trouble with this concept, consider them and the processes as metaphorical. You will achieve the same results.

lifetimes. Sometimes it's easy to learn a lesson and move on, but more often, the soul remains stuck on the same issue, struggling with it lifetime after lifetime, like a needle stuck in a record groove. These lessons show up for us all the time.

The lessons often take the form of recurrent annoyances. Your Higher Self is presenting them to you so you can resolve them satisfactorily *this* time. Instead of getting angry or avoiding them, you can release them by discovering the cause of your reaction, by facing your own unconscious or unresolved flaws, such as greed, impatience, jealousy, fear, or anger, or by dissolving the past life hook that still twists inside you.

For example, instead of reacting in a hostile manner to someone who irritates you, you might realize that he or she is providing you with an opportunity to look at the cause of your reaction. By acting as your mirror, the person helps you get rid of the charge between you and him or her, and clears the issue itself in this life. This brings you one step closer to achieving balance and healing.

Karmic issues, on the other hand, are not annoying pricks; these major problems require serious internal adjustment to be resolved, often by healing the past life that caused the karma and paying the debt (see Chapter 9). For that you need help and support. You can't do it alone. Luckily, assistance is available from many high-level resources more than eager to help you on your journey.

Higher Self

The first of these resources is your own Higher Self, whose help is integral to changework.

In the first chapter I mentioned the Inner Child part of you (aged two–eleven), the symbol of the emotional body (helpless, scared, desperate for love). The Higher Self, your wise, immortal soul that oversees your life, is far different in makeup and outlook. It sees you clearly (warts and all), knows everything about you, and wants nothing more than your greater well-being. Each one of your lifetimes has its own Higher Self, which are fragments of your Oversoul, with direct access to the Oversoul itself, and the Godhead.

The Higher Self lives above your head, far enough away from the physical body to hear divine wisdom clearly. It acts as the bridge between the Godhead and your other bodies, providing that you can hear its messages without interference or judgment, particularly from your mind, which constantly judges, analyzes, argues, comments, and just never shuts up! Meditation or some other practice that stills your mind's chatter allows you to hear your Higher Self's quiet, clear voice.

Sometimes you acquire a significant insight about something that seems impossible to know, given the information available. In those instances, the Higher Self has managed to slide an intuition past your ever-watchful mind and provide you with the information you need to make a wise, though not informed, decision (informed and wise are *not* the same).

The intrusion of someone else's energy between your Higher Self and you—by tampering with your seventh chakra (the chakra at the top of your head that looks toward the Higher Self)—can obstruct your connection with your Higher Self. The most common intruders are your parents, who have blocked the seventh chakra for control when you were a child. Though done unconsciously, its unwitting effect is to teach you that your only source of wisdom is your parents; therefore, you forget your connection to your Higher Self and your own wisdom.

More karmically dangerous are spiritual intruders—the gurus and teachers who impose control over their students. Among them are the creators of cults or sects, fundamentalists, and other religious fanatics. Evolved teachers encourage you to think for yourself and view things from a different perspective, often by using humor to jolt you out of your mental rut, and giving you both experiences and time to make your own decisions. Such a person helps you find your own wisdom and brings you in touch with your Higher Self.

Other spiritual leaders are not so enlightened; they want followers. They don't encourage independent thinking or access to higher wisdom, nor do they have your best interests at heart. Their purpose is control, and the most effective method is to cut you off from your Higher Self by putting an energy cord into your seventh chakra so you get only their information. Their victims/students are truly "brainwashed."

Until you cut that cord, you will not be able to access your Higher Self. That is one of the reasons why you can be "blind" to any other perspective. Unless your teacher gives you permission, you cannot see anything else.

On the other hand, some people do not want to hear their own inner wisdom; they want someone else's wisdom. They gladly give away their power to whomever will take it.

When others take over control of your seventh chakra, or block you from your Higher Self, they can convince you that you are unworthy of divine love, except as they decree. This belief is *completely false*. Your Higher Self and the Godhead always love you. No matter what kinds of arguments your mind concocts to discourage you ("No one will love me if they find out about the 'real me'"), they are all untrue. They serve only to make you feel even more isolated and in need of outside guidance and care (gladly provided by many cult leaders).

We tend to imagine ourselves as incomparably worse sinners than we actually are, with our normal human tendencies, good and bad. That belief was programmed into us as children, when we tried to get our own needs fulfilled. If we were unsuccessful, and most of us were, we decided we were unworthy of love and compassion.

Many of us then feel ashamed to face our Higher Self, believing that we will be judged harshly for our failings. Quite the opposite. You need to remember that your Higher Self *really does* know you, inside and out. If only you will give it a chance, your Higher Self would like to shower you with love, just as the Godhead would.

31

Your Higher Self is the most important partner you can have in changework. Not being influenced by outsiders, or your mind, or overwhelmed by your fears and needs, it can guide you through the arcane and convoluted territory known as the unconscious, to the exact memory with which you need to work, and bring you safely through the process, especially if you do not have a conscious childhood memory of the trauma.

Even if you remember these painful happenings, you may have difficulty facing them at a deep inner level for fear that what gets dredged up might be too overwhelming (that is a feeling your Inner Child holds). Your Higher Self has no such qualms. It knows how much you really can handle (and you'll be amazed at how much that is). Besides, it knows what the payoff will be—wisdom, healing, acceptance, and love.

Love is always available to you; it is you who cut yourself off from its blessings. By connecting with your Higher Self, you begin raising your self-esteem, and accepting your birthright of unconditional and unstinting love. Once you can feel the love your Higher Self dearly wants to give you, it becomes easier for you to accept it from others, both human and divine. You begin to feel safe enough to reclaim lost parts of yourself—such as your self-esteem and your sense of empowerment—you allow yourself to feel the divine love you deserve to receive from the Godhead.

How does the Higher Self help you?

- The Higher Self is dispassionate, compassionate, and wise, seeing you without judgment.

- The Higher Self, being detached from your personality, can give you perspective on what's happening—if you allow yourself to hear it.

- The Higher Self serves as the loving mediator between divine wisdom and you.

- The Higher Self, knowing everything that has happened to you, can guide you into those deep, unconscious places of pain and anguish.

- The Higher Self always has your best interests at heart. Not one other person has that, including your parents.

- The Higher Self can help you recognize and release karmic issues, and complete unfinished business.

- In every instance where the Higher Self participates in the healing process, it gives support, stability, and strength to your work.

Case Study: Jenny was a compulsive overeater. In one session, she asked her Higher Self to take her to the cause of her overeating. A memory suddenly flashed into her mind of her mother screaming at Jenny for not finishing her meal; she said she worked herself to the bone to provide food for her children, who were ungrateful and uncaring. Jenny began to eat compulsively from then on, for she had figured out that her mother would love her only if she cleaned her plate. (The trigger may sound trivial, but the implications of not eating for Jenny meant withheld love.)

With her Higher Self's help, Jenny began to reprogram her memory by calling on divine forgiveness for not finishing her food. As a result, her compulsive overeating disappeared, for her inner goad no longer pricked her whenever she left food on the plate. Later on, Jenny learned that her mother, who grew up poor and hungry in the Depression, equated lack of food with lack of love, and vowed always to provide enough food for her children. (Isn't it amazing how motives get misinterpreted down through the generations?)

The Higher Self is also essential for any past life work. You might feel a little embarrassed about what you see when you make the past life journey, or whether you will even see anything. You just have to be receptive and let your Higher Self do its job of guiding you to the pertinent event. Your Higher Self can also explain the lessons learned (or not) from the past lifetime, and any karmic debts outstanding and due.

In every phase of changework, the Higher Self is your trusted, loving, and wise guide. Without it, your work can be much harder and sometimes scarier—with it, you may begin to realize that you are no longer alone in the world.

Besides the Higher Self, there are other resources you can call on for help.

Guardian Angel

Most religious or spiritual traditions teach the concept of Guardian Angels or Guardians. Even if you do not come from such a tradition, believing in a guardian of some type that can support you is very comforting.

Your guardian angel is a being who has chosen to attach itself to you as your invisible companion. We each have one, or even several guardian angels, depending on our needs and desires. Like your Higher Self, it has your best interests at heart, but unlike your Higher Self, it is not part of your Oversoul.

Sometimes we know them—they are people who loved us while they were alive, like grandparents, who watch over us again in discarnate form. Usually, they are souls like us but bodiless at this time, who will earn extra karmic points for helping us in our life work.

Like your Higher Self, your guardian angel also provides wise suggestions, but its major purpose is to protect and help you in your work. (Just as your Higher Self has a hard time getting through to you, so does your Guardian Angel.) Having a guardian angel is almost as valuable as having your Higher Self—but not quite. Though your Higher Self always speaks your own wisdom, your guardian angel only has its wisdom to give you, not yours—and your own wisdom is always best.

Children are very much in tune with the idea of guardian angels, who help them maneuver through their young lives and provide loving companionship. In fact, those invisible friends children talk to are usually their guardian angels.

Angels

Finally you can call on angels. Angels are light beings of a much higher order who are part of the Godhead and do its will. There are an infinite number of angels who at your summons will gladly lend a hand in your life. They do not remain with you for any extended period of time unless it is necessary, but instead, they come when needed. When you are doing changework and you want some extra high-level assistance, angels bring both divine power and divine blessing into your process.

You may feel comforted knowing that you always can call on an angel for help in releasing your problem—or you may feel a self-imposed unworthiness that argues that you shouldn't presume to call upon them. Nonsense! Angels help; they do not judge your worth. That is not their purpose or essence. Judgment is a low vibration, far lower than angel essence, and in their presence it dissolves away, although since you have so much self-judgment inside of you, more will manifest again after they have departed. Eventually, if you work to acknowledge and accept angelic love, all your judgment energies will dissipate.

We can call on the archangels as well as the regular angelic foot soldiers. This is very important when something comes up that terrifies you. Having someone of the stature of Archangel Michael to protect or defend you from childhood abusers is enormously reassuring. Michael wields a sharp sword that can quite effectively chop out toxic energies or drive away evil or unwanted people. He and his archangelic counterparts are always available for special healing assignments.

Not being part of you like the Higher Self, or discarnate souls like the guardian angels, angelic forces speak with divine authority. That means they can heal your karmic issue instantly, if they feel you have atoned enough, or let you finish working it out in this lifetime.

> **Case Study:** Leon discovered that he had endured particularly bad childhood physical abuse because he had run a boys' school in a previous lifetime where he starved and brutalized his young charges. He chose this life to atone for that behavior. Leon asked his Higher Self for help in dissolving the karma, but his Higher Self could not do so; it recommended that he call in an angel. The angel deemed that he had suffered enough for his previous abuse and released the residual atonement.

The following exercise helps you connect with your Higher Self. You can substitute the Guardian Angel for your Higher Self; the steps are the same.

EXERCISE

Meeting your Higher Self or Your Guardian Angel

1. Imagine a special place—a room furnished as you want, or a lovely forest or meadow, or by a mountain or the sea. Since time and space are mutable in your imagination, you can create anything you want.

2. Ask your Higher Self to meet you there. Notice what it looks like. Higher Selves come in many shapes, sizes, and dimensions. Some may look like gods and goddesses, others may look like you. Others appear simply as energy shapes, while some can only be detected as invisible but tangible presences. There is no right or wrong form for your Higher Self, just whatever you perceive. In fact, from one session to another, the Higher Self may change shape and dimension. If you don't see or sense your Higher Self this time, you might another time, as you become more trusting and open.

3. Ask your Higher Self what it would like to say to you, and if it has a gift to give you. Your Higher Self rarely has the opportunity to speak to you directly, unimpeded by your mind. Whatever it says or gives you, no matter how odd-sounding, thank your Higher Self. If you receive a gift, ask your Higher Self how to use it. You may be surprised, once you've come back to outer reality, how insightful its message is.

4. When you're finished, open your eyes and come back, remembering that you can go back to visit your Higher Self at any time. It is always there.

Now that you have met your Higher Self, and/or your Guardian Angel, you can face your unknown and perhaps terrifying inner world with the knowledge that you aren't alone. As you do your changework, you will create a conduit between you and your Higher Self, which can block out the interference from your mind so you can receive insights that will help you evolve to reach that golden balance and harmony.

CHAPTER 4

PRESENT TIME

In order to transform the past, we need to be grounded in the present. It's like having a rope solidly anchored in rock before rappelling down a cliff face. First, however, we have to get into the present.

For many of us, the present can be an enormous surprise because we've rarely spent much time here. We are locked into our past, pulled there by all our doubts, fears, and worries. By bringing ourselves into the present, we can reduce the impact of those needs and fears and release them.

The present has always been an uncomfortable place for us—as far back as infancy, when as a child we expressed our inchoate needs for love, attention, and caring. When we were comforted, nurtured, and held, we felt contented and happy; but if we didn't get that nurturance, our lives became filled with fear and worry. As we grew older, getting those needs met still occupied our attention—even now as an adult, it colors every aspect of our lives.

Suppose you need to make a decision. Although your mind provides all sorts of logical arguments for or against it, the real decision is made with your emotional heart. This Inner Child part of us bases its decision on what will keep it safe and loved. For a good adult decision, there needs to be balance between mind and heart. The emotional heart requires the mind's perspicacity, perspective, and acumen—tempered with the wisdom of the Higher Self, and clear communication among them, unfettered by childhood fears. That comes when you get unstuck from the past and let your adult resources govern your life. Bringing yourself into the present will make it much easier to let go of some of the inner blocks that prevent you from using all of your faculties.

Present Time

Let's begin with present time. Are you in the present? Or are parts of you stuck somewhere else? If your childhood patterns are controlling you, if you are locked into a certain belief system, or if you live in fear of some sort, you aren't in present time. Your past or your future (based on past fears) governs you.

Many of us remain trapped by some event(s) that occurred in the past. You could probably put your finger on incidents or events that changed your life. Sometimes they were wonderful, sometimes pretty horrible— or just extreme. Events like an assault, rape, or sexual abuse, or some kind of endangerment qualify. Everything in your life since then has been colored by that defining moment. You cannot ignore its consequences in your life. Moreover, every time you think of it, you trap energy in it. That energy becomes inaccessible for other purposes and lowers your vibration. It's like turning a molehill into a mountain; remember how relieved you felt when you found out that a problem wasn't as large as you had feared after all.

To reclaim that energy, you need to free yourself from the control of those memories. Using changework, the energy trapped in them gets freed up (like an inheritance that suddenly becomes available).

Before that happens, it helps immensely to bring yourself—your aura, physical body, mind, and heart—into present time, by creating what I call the "present time field." Breaking free of the bonds of the past takes work, but it's much easier if you are inside the present time field, which brings any energy from past events into the present, and raises your vibrations (see Chapter 5).

For example, if as a child you were beaten by your father, you're holding on to a lot of energy around those memories; and whenever you remember it, more of your energy gets trapped. It's like a grain of sand irritating an oyster's soft body. To protect itself, the oyster wraps the sand with a nacreous coating to soothe the irritation. Unable to be expelled, the grain not only remains, but its presence inside the oyster increases with every coat. That's what happens when you keep ruminating over personal trauma. Your energy accretions accumulate, but unlike the oyster, who gets a pearl at the end, your energy gets trapped in a kind of black hole, which also traps your energy.

When you bring those accretions into present time, since they have only a connection to the past event, they leave. It's like rinsing the mud off your boots after you have been splashing through a puddle. Your boots are the incident, and the mud is the accretion. Although the core issue may remain, the angst built up around it goes down the drain for the present, or until you have built up the resources to let it go permanently.

> **Case Study:** Desiree held an image of her family responsibility as a ton of clay piled on her back. The more she thought about her responsibility, the worse she felt, and the less able she was to face it, much less handle it. After a while, she could barely contemplate the whole issue. When she brought it into present time, she saw (and felt) the heavy burden slide off her back and break into pieces on the ground.

Bringing her image into present time released all the energy trapped around it (like guilt, anger, frustration, anger). She still needed to work on her responsibility issue, but it was no longer encumbered by all the accretions that glued it into place. Moreover, releasing the trapped energy deflated the responsibility to its original size, which, though overwhelming for a kid, was manageable enough for an adult.

Once accretions are removed (common ones like parental accusations, personal guilt, or judgments), you can focus on the core issue. Otherwise, you'll have to spend long, tedious sessions processing through the accretions until you can reach the issue itself.

The present time field also exposes any foreign energies stuck inside you, very often your parents' energies. By bringing yourself into the present, anything that doesn't belong to you can no longer remain. It can be quite a shock to discover how much of the emotional baggage you tote around belongs to other people. It's time to send it back to its owners.

Changework

Before starting any changework, you need to do two preliminary techniques—*Defining Your Space* and *Retrieving Your Energy*. Both of these exercises do basic cleanout and are essential for all other processes, for they make your work much easier.

Defining Your Space

By defining the edges of your aura (the eighteen inches around your body), you create a personal boundary that declares, "This is my space. I belong here, and everybody else belongs out there." It's not a line in the sand, but a flexible force field that simply delineates your territory. It does not isolate you from others since you can choose to let special friends inside—as you always have. You create a home where you can be yourself and work on your issues. Otherwise, your present time field cannot be fully effective. When you create the present time field, you may discover that you've been sharing a 3x3 room with everyone you've ever known, so there's no room for you. Some of these people you may actually not mind having there, but they need to be invited by you at your choice. Other people you may not want there at all. They may be drinking or addiction buddies from years ago, and since then you've gone through recovery. Yet there they are, still sitting in your space, enticing you with the next hit or line or drink. Their presence brings your energy down whenever you fight against the urge to use. Or you might find in your space all the judgmental people who have criticized you all your life. There may also be people who've made you feel uncomfortable, and who hang onto you.

It's time to put an end to this party. Dig out the guests who have fallen asleep on your bed, the ones talking in the living room, and the ones rummaging through your refrigerator, hand them their coats, shoo them out the door, and send them home—out of your space. Many people feel very strange after doing this; they are suddenly alone after years of being unwitting hosts to a multitude of people.

The most important reason for defining your space, however, is self-love. You cannot love others until you feel safe enough to love yourself, and you can feel love only in your space. It's like a treasured friend phoning you to say, "I love you." When you're not at home to take the call, you can't get the message. Only when you come back to your home can you receive it. How wonderful it feels hearing those words! If you're lost in the past and out of your body, you can't receive this gift.

Finally, if you aren't in your body, changework will become more difficult—not impossible—but harder than necessary. You won't be able to access your resources easily, particularly since blocks cut you off from your

Higher Self's wisdom. The present time field releases foreign energies and mental blocks, so you resume communication with your Higher Self.

EXERCISES

Defining Your Space

Before you can do any work on clearing out people from your space, you have to define it—which means setting up boundaries between yourself and the world. That is not only a protection for you, but also a reassurance that you have a presence here on the planet.

1. Focus your attention on your aura—your invisible energy shield. Ask that it cover you from over your head to underneath your feet, and spread out 18 inches around you. Feel what it's like being in your very own space.

2. To clean unwanted alien energies from your space, imagine a large golden comb with 18-inch teeth. Use it to comb out your aura, like you're combing your own hair, from head to toe. Physically run your hands up and down your body in a combing motion, holding the psychic comb in your hand.

3. Pull all alien energies from your space so whatever is inside belongs to you and no one else. Let the combed-out energies fall onto the earth, where they can be absorbed. You may feel some strange sensations in your body as you do this exercise, or soon afterward. After all, just having your own energy in your space is quite unusual.

45

4. Imagine a very large gold ball of light above your head. Let it slide down into your body and spread its healing light out to the edges of your aura. This gold energy defines the limits of your space and raises your vibration so that no one with a lower vibration can invade you easily (see Chapter 5), or push you out of your space—not your parents, lover, or others—without your permission.

Retrieving Your Energy

Since alien energy is stuck in your aura from both recent and long-past interactions, it's only reasonable to assume that you left some of your energy in other places, as well.

In fact, your energy is spread out all over the place—stuck in people's auras, left in all the places you've lived and worked, and locked in the past. This next technique brings some of your essence back to you.

1. Close your eyes and imagine you have an energy whistle, like an ultra-high-pitched dog whistle. Blow it to call your own energy home (and no one else's).

2. After a few moments, the pieces of energy will start flowing back to you; they may appear or feel like snowflakes, blobs, a river of energy or light or any other form you might imagine. As your body and aura start absorbing your returning essence, you may even begin to feel like you have more shape and presence.

3. Give yourself about five minutes to allow your energy to come back. The first time you do this, you

might discover energies coming back from years ago. You'll know because you'll get odd recollections from long-past incidents.

Do both of these exercises every day for maximum benefit. As you continue doing them, energies that have been missing since earliest childhood will return, until finally you are more complete than you have been in ages. Once you have retrieved your energy, you're ready to take the next step.

Setting Up a Present Time Field

Creating a present time field requires nothing more than your imagination, and the postulation (not even the belief) that this technique works. You may or may not notice any body reaction as you do the technique, but there will be shifts in your energy. If you feel a jolt, that's your four bodies adjusting and realigning to the newly accessible energies.

Creating a present time field before every change-work session helps you process much more easily. The two techniques described work equally well.

The Wand

1. Imagine a gold wand, in whatever shape and form you want. Pick it up and hold it. (See it resting in your hand. Imagine your fingers curved around it.) This is a present time wand. (You may have your eyes closed or open, whichever feels best for you.)

2. Touch any part of your body or aura with it. Whatever you touch comes into present time.

3. Because the aura has seven layers, tap at least seven times in various areas of your aura.

4. Tap the seven main chakras (see pp. 111–112 for further discussion of chakra system).

5. Tap your feet and hands (which have their own chakras and help with the movement of energy through your body).

6. Tap your Higher Self, which is 6–8 inches above your head. You have now brought all of you into present time.

The Veil

1. Imagine a shimmering golden veil in front of you, between you and your destination.

2. Stand up very slowly, and, mindfully, step through the veil, as if you were walking through a waterfall, letting its energies sluice through you. Because it has very high energy, it cannot be pushed aside by your dense physical body. As you step through the veil, it will bathe all your cells with present time, bringing all of your bodies and memories into present time, and releasing old trapped energies.

You can do these techniques at any time. The more often you do them, the more of you comes into present time for release. As you proceed, you will discover that many of your issues fall into one of three categories. These are the core issues that rule your life. (They will be discussed in greater detail in Chapter 15.)

CHAPTER 5

ENERGY
VIBRATIONS

Until now, you have been operating at a fairly low vibration. All the parts of you are out of balance and out of tune with yourself. Once you chose to live on this planet, you encountered experiences in the course of your life that knocked you further off balance. Yet that was part of your master plan—to retune yourself according to the experiences and lessons you have here on this planet. To do that, you need to familiarize yourself with the qualities of energy.

Energy consists of two elements—vibration and frequency level.

Vibrations: Sound and Clarity

Vibration is a quality indicating the clarity of your energy. It gives off a tone or pitch. A muddy tone indicates blockage in your energy, while a clearer pitch indicates more free-flowing energy with fewer blocks. The pitch is also governed by the kind of blocks you have, which indicate the kind of energy you emanate. Other people can detect when you are sending out good or bad vibrations, and you can feel theirs as well.

What do vibrations have to do with changework? Everything inside of you is interconnected. When you raise your vibration, or frequency, you shake up all those parts of you that do not vibrate at that level. It's like sending ultrasound into a kidney stone; the sound waves break up the stone so it can pass out of your body. That's what vibrations do.

Your vibration is enhanced by emotional intensity. The stronger the emotion you express, the more intense your vibration. A lot of people believe that the more enlightened you become, the less intensity you will have. That is incorrect. It's not the intensity that is important, but its clarity.

Somebody who's very impassioned about something feels intense; if he's expressing joy, we feel uplifted, excited, enlivened, and energized. On the other hand, somebody who spews rage or hatred is just as passionate, but his intensity makes us feel dirty, disturbed, or uncomfortable. I can't listen to rap music for that reason. The energy coming out of those songs is so full of rage that it literally hurts my body. I don't want this kind of vibration in my space.

Having such a strong, hurtful feeling inside you means that your energy is trapped and cannot flow freely. It's as though you're stuck in a pressure cooker, and as you get more and more enraged, your vibration intensifies—with no outlet for release—except through an explosion. The subsequent emotion feels excruciatingly painful and unpleasant—like stabbing knives. It is also extremely damaging to your physical health over a long period of time.

Body Vibrations

Besides your overall vibration, each of your bodies has its own vibratory sound, with the physical body having the lowest frequency, and the soul, the highest. Together, these different tones form a musical chord, creating a deep, rich tone that combines the different frequencies together into a beautiful, complex, balanced harmony.

If you could hear the vibrations from your different bodies, you would also hear the clarity or muddiness of each one's sound. Your Higher Self always vibrates at a lovely pitch; but your other bodies may sound sour because of the blocks in each of them. When the muck has been removed, their clear energies will combine to create a balanced harmony. It's a state few of our bodies have attained, but it can be reached occasionally. There may come a time when you achieve it all the time. Even as you get close to that balance, you can feel the difference in yourself.

When you find that delicate balance where the bodies create the perfect harmonic chord, it feels wonderful—joyful, expansive, and healing. Whenever you fall out of harmony you can sense it instantly.

Being in that perfect vibration means everything moves clearly and smoothly. Your consciousness expands; you feel lighter and more joyous; you see yourself and the world more clearly and lovingly; you feel

51

more empathy for others; and you perceive new perspectives. (If we had more people vibrating at the gold harmony level, the world would be far different.)

Frequency Levels

When you get depressed, you have much less energy available than when you are active. Your level drops as your energy becomes trapped or immobile. If you are chronically depressed, not only do you have low energy, you are also loaded with negative feelings that pull you down and cause your energy to be trapped—which makes you feel worse, and pulls your energy down more. It's a vicious cycle.

Your work, your attitudes, and the people in your life (business and personal) both create and affect the level, as well as the quality, of your vibrations. When you were first born, you vibrated at a very high level (you are, after all, a cosmic being inhabiting a body). Then, all through childhood, your family assaulted you with disapproval, rage, manipulation, guilt, judgment, blame, or neglect, which distorted and blocked your feelings, and clogged your aura with their energies. The stronger their emotions and the younger you were, the less ability you had to dispel them. Gradually, they brought down your energy level so that you ended up vibrating at a level that reflected your belief about your self-worth (or lack of it), and the world reinforced that idea—then and now.

If you believe you are not very good, it's as though you carry a body shield in front of you projecting the message, "I only deserve to have experiences that prove I'm not very good." You then create situations that reinforce that message. If you are in an abusive relationship, your vibrations have attracted that kind of person into your life. The lower your vibration, the worse the energies, experiences, and relationships you create for yourself.

Take codependency. If you are codependent, you have an inner feeling of negative self-worth, and an unfulfilled need for love that you hope will be satisfied by helping others (but it never really is enough). That codependent behavior traps you in guilt and obligation. As a result, you endeavor to give away your energy to others, leaving very little for yourself. Your vibration is muddy.

For things to change, you must demolish the old structure. Think of a tent held up with eight stakes. As each support gives way, the tent puts more stress on the others. As you keep pulling out stakes, it becomes more difficult for the tent to remain erect; finally, it falls over because the stakes that are left cannot handle the intense pressure. That's what happens with change-work. Each time you do the exercises in this book, you pull out another bolt that holds you to your past (although you have far more than eight anchor bolts holding you down).

At times you may believe that you'll never get to the bottom of a particular issue, but eventually, with enough work, it gets released. It's like cleaning up a large wet stain. As you wipe off one area, the colored liquid over-runs it, but the stain is slightly weaker than it was before. With every spongeful of liquid removed, you reduce the stain's strength, bit by bit, until finally it's gone.

Every time you raise your vibration, you drive away or eliminate some segment of the toxic energies inside you. When you break that codependent need for others' approval and allow yourself to be nurtured, you raise your energy level and your vibration. As a result, you have so much energy, love, and joy that you gladly share it with others—not from lack and need and a hope of getting something back, but from abundance.

Higher Frequency

The most important effect of raising your vibrational frequency is that the structures inside you that don't match your new vibration must change as well. It's like riding a ten-speed bike. When you shift the gears on your handlebars, you force the gears on the wheel to move as well. They can't argue with you; they shift or the bike breaks down.

This is why whenever you do changework, it is impossible to regress. It can be very scary because your conscious desire for change may be coupled with an equally great fear from your four non-spiritual bodies, for whom change is terrifying. It helps if you let them adjust gradually to the loss of old patterns and the reclamation of old energies. That means a steady process of change-work over time, not wholesale demolition and recon-struction. I find when I do my own growth work that I must stop for a while and let the changes be absorbed and assimilated throughout my bodies; then I continue.

As these changes occur, and as old negative energies vanish from your life, you begin to vibrate at a higher frequency, so that whatever and whoever falls below your vibration cannot gravitate toward you. It's as though you have disappeared from their radar—you're invisible to them. Instead, you attract new relationships and accept new attitudes about yourself and others that are different from what you knew before, sometimes markedly so. That can be unnerving because at first the new relationships are unfamiliar. The higher you vibrate, the more of your Self you have, so the more of your energy is available for your healing.

Gold (the love energy) resonates at the highest vibration of all, followed by silver. That means whenever you fill yourself with gold, it breaks up and flushes away anything that vibrates at a lower pitch.

Sickness

Under normal circumstances, your reserve of energy is barely half of what you were born with (because your available energy is locked away in your traumas), but when you get sick, you have only a small amount of energy available, since your body is using it to fight off the illness. Any kind of activity uses it up immediately. That's why you need to rest—to regain your energy.

Temporary sicknesses like flu and colds serve as one of the body's most efficient mechanisms for cleaning out clogged energies and raising our vibrations. (The particular variety of sickness tells you where most of your blockage is: heart = chest colds, bronchitis; communication = head colds, sore throat, coughs.)

In the seventies, I used to tell friends that I got a cold when I needed to clean out my energy system. They all laughed at me and called it a coincidence. After a while, when I started correlating their illnesses to their energy blocks, they admitted that I might be correct. Now it's common knowledge.

Working with higher beings also helps you raise your vibration level. When you allow your Higher Self or an angel's energy into your body, you vibrate at a much higher pitch. Sometimes you can accept it, and sometimes it creates enormous chaos inside you if your energy is low. The more you can allow yourself to absorb these higher vibrational energies, the more you will raise your vibration.

Vibration Scale

Imagine an energy scale that goes from 0–10 (below). A zero is complete evil, the worst kind of low life controlled by elementals and evil spirits—your own "hell" on earth. A 10 means you are at the level of transcendence. It is a divine place to sit for about a minute—and that's it! Your body cannot tolerate a vibration that is too far beyond its capability, and could self-destruct if left up there too long. Luckily, it will pull your vibration back down to a bearable level almost immediately.

0	1	2	3	4	5	6	7	8	9	10
Dead – Hell	Horrible	Pretty Bad	Lower	Normal	Comfortable	Good	Better	High	Very High	Dead – Bliss

Raising your energy without clearing the blocks can hurt you physically, and may trigger a quick cold as your body tries to raise its vibration to compensate. You must clear out your psychic pores before you move your dial much higher. The present time field will help you by releasing a lot of those energies.

The best way to raise your vibration is by doing it slowly and gradually. It's like dieting; crash diets take off lots of weight fast, but soon the pounds creep back. For real long-term reduction, the best programs work slowly and methodically, accustoming you and your body to the changes gradually. It's the same thing with vibrations. That's why I recommend raising the dial one notch at a time, until you find a comfortable level.

Even if you are pretty clear, and you can tolerate a higher dial setting, there is another problem—few people can match that vibration. The higher your vibration, the more difficult it is for people below that frequency to interact with you. If you can only attract what is at your level and above, you'll end up alone. (How many 10s do you know? I guarantee, none. They can't survive at that level.) For some bliss and few friends, try eight. In order to keep your friends and family in your life, a range of 5–6 is the best. You can communicate with most people; it's a safe level for personal healing, and it helps raise the vibrations of others around you.

Anyone below that level cannot bother or harm you because your vibration is too high for them—the exception is paying back karma.

EXERCISES

Body Alignment

This exercise aligns your four mortal bodies with your Higher Self, so that they all vibrate at the same pitch, even if only for a few moments. Don't do this exercise in your mind. Actually move around.

1. You need four seats, two objects, like pillows or stuffed animals, and an afghan or shawl. Take two objects and put them on two of the seats.

2. Sit down at a third seat, wrapping the afghan around you. Clean out your aura and put yourself in present time.

3. The afghan or shawl is your aura, which you will now take off. Say, "I'm taking off my aura and leaving it here," as you drop the shawl onto the seat. Do this slowly and mindfully.

4. Now, go to the first pillow, pick it up, and sit down. Say, "I am leaving my emotional body here," and imagine it filling the pillow. Stand up and put the pillow back down on the seat.

5. Go to the next pillow, pick it up, and sit down. Say, "I am leaving my mental body here," and imagine it going into the pillow. Stand up and put the pillow back down on the seat.

6. Go to the last seat (no pillow) and sit down. This is your physical body.

7. Ask your Higher Self to align the body's energy with it. Imagine your Higher Self sliding down through the top of your head and filling your body up with its presence. *You don't have to do anything; just sit there and let your Higher Self do its job.* Your body will be vibrating at a level you haven't experienced for many years. If you start feeling aches and pains, your body is letting you know about places where it's blocked. (This exercise can help show you where to focus your changework as in Chapter 7.)

8. After a few moments, stand up. Your Higher Self and physical body are in alignment. Move over to the mental body, pick up the pillow, and sit down; hug the pillow. Call the mental body back inside you for the Higher Self to put into alignment.

9. Your mental body may make all sorts of comments while your Higher Self does its work. Acknowledge any comments that come up (simply say, "Thank you") and continue working, whether you believe it's effective or not.

10. Repeat the procedure with the emotional body. Let the Higher Self put it into alignment.

11. Sit down in your aura. Put the shawl or afghan around your body while your Higher Self aligns your energies. (You might find it extremely difficult to hold the alignment for more than a few moments. That shows how blocked you are. Or you might find it quite comfortable because you've done some work on yourself.)

12. To strengthen and add healing to the process, imagine a gold ball of sunlight coming down through the top of your head and filling up your body and aura. This gold energy reprograms your cells for love and joy instead of the low vibrations you have absorbed in the past.

13. Open your eyes when you are ready.

Every time you do that exercise, you vibrate at that higher essence level, and all of you—body, soul, mind, and heart, blend together in the way you were supposed to be on this planet.

Vibrational Armor

When you were born, you came onto the planet clean and pure, free of the blocks and accretions you carry around with you as an adult. These form a kind of psychic armor that lowers your vibrations. Imagine a clean and shiny ship ready to be launched, and beside it, another one pulled into drydock, encrusted with barnacles, corroded, and rusty from oxidation. That is how your invisible adult exoskeleton looks. Wouldn't it be nice to get rid of it and start all over again with something new—free of rigidity, corrosion, and constriction? You need some protection for yourself, but it can be something with a far higher vibration.

1. Imagine you are wearing armor—heavy, impenetrable, firm, and hard to walk around in. That's what you carry around all the time. It provides you with protection, as well as constricting your movements.

2. Tap your body with the present time wand to bring your armor into present time.

3. Take your armor off, piece by piece, and drop it on the ground with a clatter. Then step away from it. Actually, moving from one spot to another on your floor makes this exercise more tangible. When you look back, you can see (or sense) your armor lying on the ground.

4. The original high vibration energy envelope that your baby self came in still exists in the very center of your heart. Take the energy envelope out of your heart.

5. It's an enormously flexible, baby-sized body suit. Climb into it. It will expand. Pull it on over your feet and legs, arms and hands, up your torso and shoulders, over your head and face, until it covers all of you.

6. Dispose of your old armor. You can break it apart with a hammer, throw it in the ocean, drop it into a vat of gold liquid, have it hauled away by cosmic garbage trucks. You don't need it any longer.

This new suit will protect you with the highest cosmic vibrations, free of personal contamination.

Raising Vibrations

1. Imagine a dial that goes from 0 to 10. It may have smaller gradations if you want. Ask your Higher Self to show you where your dial is set.

2. Reach out and raise the dial a notch. That means if you are at a 4, raise it to a 5. If that feels uncomfortable, raise it half a notch to 4.5.

3. Check it occasionally to make sure that the dial setting stays at that level. When you feel more comfortable, raise it a little higher. Don't go beyond 6, at least until you have done a lot of clearing work.

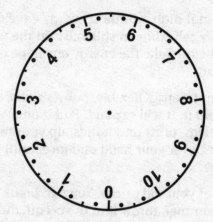

Having done all this preparatory work in the first five chapters, it is time to begin the actual changework process of healing the past.

• • •

CHAPTER 6

IMAGES: THE MIND

Imagine your belief system as the steel girders of a building inside your mind that hold and control the attitudes that color your perceptions and conceptions of yourself and your world. Belief systems shape your life. Some are moral or ethical systems of right and wrong, like the Ten Commandments or the Golden Rule, or tenets of a particular group such as those that define you as Jewish, Christian, or Muslim, and further, as an Orthodox vs. Reform or Conservative Jew. Other beliefs are centered on a particular country or doctrine, organization, or attitude (like "The American Way," "democracy," "intellectualism," "feminism," etc.).

Two belief systems collide when both sides refuse to give up their own beliefs or let another in (like environmentalism vs. growth). The more rigid your belief system is, the less ability you have for flexible thinking, empathy, or understanding others. Fundamentalists believe in a black-and-white world, while other people encourage shades of gray.

Beliefs

We have two kinds of beliefs—macro and micro beliefs. Macro systems encompass large values—moral, governmental, religious, philosophical codes. There's a story about a man unknowingly cursed by a witch doctor. When the man learned of the curse some years later, he died within three days. Why? His tribal (macro) belief system accepted that being cursed meant death, regardless of any rational arguments to the contrary.

Micro systems are person-centered, arising from family beliefs and personal experience. Just as you chose the behaviors that would give you the love and safety you needed in your family from an early age, you absorbed your family's belief system as well. Having learned what values were acceptable in your home, and in the world around you, you incorporated them into your own belief structure.

If your father beat you, you may believe such abuse is not only an acceptable way of dealing with family issues, but even an expression of love. Or perhaps you were told by a parent or adult to allow other children to play with your toys (whether you wanted to or not); it was supposed to teach you about sharing—and inadvertently taught you about deservability (you don't deserve possessions). Such beliefs can be very pernicious; you may accept them blindly and without consideration because they are the only experience you have.

Although some belief systems appear pretty obvious (usually macro beliefs), micro beliefs are often both subtle and unconscious. You usually don't realize that you think and act according to them until something brings them into your consciousness—like being hauled off to jail for beating your wife.

If you were born in a world that appeared unsafe, the message you received was, "I have no right to be alive." If you were neglected, you got the message, "I don't deserve love." If you had an over-doting parent who smothered you, your message was, "I have no right to be myself." All of these messages created a core belief that said, "I am no good." Everything in your life then reinforced it.

Belief systems get cemented into your world view, first by family attitudes, later by religion and school, but mostly by television shows, which continually emphasize one viewpoint or other. The "Leave It to Beaver" family—wife at home in dress and pearls, husband working—reinforced the value system of white middle-class America of the 1950s. That particular image has been thrown onto the garbage heap, as new values (both good and bad) have replaced it.

We tend to take on our parents' belief system as our own. They have given us a framework with which to build our own system—but if we either adopt their whole system or reject it, unless we sift through their values and discover what is right for us, we are not being true to ourselves. If they've done their job well, we can recognize what works for us, what feels right, and what doesn't have value any longer.

Every single decision you make reflects your belief system. If you believe you must look and act a certain way, you will. If you believe you are at the mercy of your body and mind, you are. If you hold an image of yourself as worthless, you will create worthlessness in your life. If you believe you don't deserve success, then you won't create it. Any argument to the contrary will be dismissed and devalued with comments (voiced or unvoiced) like "If you really knew me...." Forming an abusive relationship only reinforces your bad-self image.

Changing Beliefs

Think of your belief system as a collection of patterns that allows you to order and view the world, and also obstruct your view, like a series of screens between you and the world. When you look through a screen door, you don't see a clear picture of what's outside; your view is obscured slightly by the mesh. Although your mind is aware of the screen, you usually ignore its presence, but if you had ten different screens in ten different shades and patterns in front of your eyes, it would be much more difficult to discern anything clearly through them. That is precisely what happens with your belief system. Its screens obfuscate some areas and give you tunnel vision in others.

When you adopt a belief system, you accept a whole set of conditions that limit the possibilities in your life. Depending on its rigidity, it's hard to see a different perspective, much less comprehend it. The stronger the conviction, the more energy it takes to hold that belief in place and drive away all the others.

Because beliefs control your perceptions, they are almost impossible to change without some serious, dedicated work. It means you have to drop your screens, one by one, to give you more access to different viewpoints. Each time that happens, you can no longer look at an issue in the same old way—and in so doing, you release trapped energy and raise your vibration.

Sometimes you find yourself having an unusual insight; you feel a sense of strangeness, of dislocation, of being lost without familiar beacons. You may choose to explore that feeling, for it's a message from your Higher Self, offering you an alternative viewpoint. Or you may push this message away and forget about it because it doesn't fit into your accepted world view. This is the most common reaction.

In Chapter 2 I talked about enlightened teachers who encourage us to examine our beliefs from an odd or unexpected perspective. When we do so, we expand ourselves; we no longer make decisions from limited criteria, but from a larger perspective. Otherwise, we will remain mentally stagnant.

Let's take something as explosive as the gay issue. If you are anti-gay and your son announces that he is gay, he has shaken your belief system. You can do what many parents have done, and disown him because of your moral conviction that being gay is a sin. That's the simplest option—and it leaves your belief system safe and intact. However, there are other choices and perspectives.

You may decide that 1) you'll cut your son out of your life, or 2) you'll struggle with your love for him because of his "immoral" lifestyle, either openly or within yourself, or 3) you'll say, "Although I don't condone your lifestyle, I love you anyway," or 4) you'll accept your son wholeheartedly, no matter what he is, because he is your son. Or any variation thereof.

Will you make a simple, black-and-white choice, according to your religious and moral beliefs, or will your decision be grounded in compassion, even it if violates your beliefs? Just wrestling with the issue is self-expanding, for it forces you to drop the screen that automatically rejects gays (and maybe other groups as well). Following your belief system may be "right" (within that system), but if it cuts off love, it may not necessarily be the "right thing" to do.

Jesus taught that love is the most important quality of all. If you condemn someone because of his beliefs, you are committing the same sin as if someone condemned *you* for *your* beliefs. On the other hand, when you say, "This is what I believe, but..," not only do you begin to let go of a screen, you start to release some of the energy trapped in your belief system.

It takes a lot of energy to maintain a belief. When you let it go, you cause a great shift inside. All that energy that was locked away is now available, and the dismantling of any internal structure immediately shifts your vibration and self-perspective.

Of all of your bodies, the mind is most terrified of what will happen if you get out of your comfort zone of safe beliefs. It maintains a fierce determination to defend those beliefs, no matter how rigid, and releases them only with great difficulty. When you start having unexpected thoughts and perceptions, the last thing it wants is for you to examine them; you might move out of your comfort zone and make serious changes in your life.

For example, quite typically, if an alcoholic stops drinking, the rest of the family may work strenuously to force him back to drink, no matter how destructive for everyone. Why? If one person in the family changes, everyone else who enabled the alcoholic to go on drinking may have to look at themselves and their own codependent behavior and feelings; that means they'd get pulled out of their "safe" world. For them, familiar dysfunction, though bad, is better than change.

The mind is your codependent, trying to keep you static and unchanging. It works hard to enable you to continue your addictive or dysfunctional behavior. However, when you slide a new idea into your belief system that pries it open, you begin to create a serious change in your attitudes, feelings, and beliefs—and you will not remain the same person you were. That's why your mind, your family, and your friends will try desperately to stop that process from happening. It makes them all too uncomfortable.

Religious groups usually excommunicate members of their congregation who ask questions or come to conclusions outside the accepted belief system. If you happen to live in a community where conformity, rigidity, and group thinking are emphasized, and individuality and self-reflection devalued or minimized, you may be forced to confront the ultimate choice: stay and conform, or leave the group and give up your beliefs. Your decision may turn your whole life upside down, especially if you persist in your own path.

Self-Image

The ability to change is dependent on the flexibility of your belief system, and your belief system creates the image you have of yourself. If you believe that you are no good, you have woven a self-image out of all your negative beliefs. Every time you are criticized (fairly or not), or you feel diminished in some way, you reinforce that negative self-image, and of course you shut yourself away from your Higher Self because you are convinced you are unworthy.

You form your self-image based on how people see you, what you believe about yourself, and your attitude toward others and the world. This self-image affects everything you do, feel, desire, or fear, and it affects your vibrations.

If your internal image appears worthless and unhappy, then you're going to project worthlessness and sadness.

Have you had this experience: You call your parents to crow about some major achievement in your life, and they say something like, "Yes, but...your marriage failed," or "...you don't have any children." Your self-esteem is completely deflated by their disparaging comments and your accomplishment is totally invalidated. You don't have the ability and strength to reject their injurious comments because you define yourself according to your inner image, not your accomplishments.

The comic strip "Cathy" illustrates this dynamic perfectly in her interactions with her mother. If Cathy had a stronger sense of herself, her mother's digs would roll off her back. She can't because her mother has unerringly zapped her Achilles heel, her shaky self-image.

For example, it's very difficult for women to create a healthy internal image with pictures of thin women assaulting them on television and in advertising. Women striving to match that ideal through diets often develop bulimia, anorexia, and other compulsive eating habits, to the detriment of their health and well-being, for they have accepted and internalized a flawed image of themselves as too fat (in comparison to the thin models they see).

I have worked with many women who say they're not good enough, not successful enough; in other words, they're not perfect. Their family, employers, and acquaintances perpetuate or enhance their feelings of diminishment. When they have gone inside themselves, they have discovered a negative self-image that is way out of date—and way out of balance.

Many overweight people see a very thin inner image. What better way to make themselves feel worse than by comparing themselves to an ideal that they simply cannot achieve. Not only do they mentally beat themselves up, they overindulge in food because they need to assuage their pain and misery—which continues to feed their negative self-image—and the vicious cycle continues. Every time you make your comparison and feel bad, that energy gets trapped in psychic fat cells.

Unless you have done a lot of work on yourself, you don't realize that rarely does your inner image bear any resemblance to reality. How can you see it clearly when your beliefs about yourself get in the way? Nor can you see anything else because your belief system won't let you.

> **Case Study:** Alma was overweight and depressed, with very low self-esteem (regardless of the fact that she was a highly paid manager). When she looked at her inner image, she saw a very slender woman wearing a black sheath with pearls, and a perfect coiffure unlike her limp blond mop. "This is the Ice Princess," she said, "very cold and unfeeling. Looking at her makes me feel awful because she's everything I'm not."

I asked her to get rid of the picture for exactly that reason and construct a new image of herself as she would like to look in three months. She created a picture of herself as somewhat thinner and happier than she really was. From now on, whenever she looked at this new image (not the unlamented Ice Princess), she could make a self-comparison without feeling guilt or shame.

That three-month leeway gave her the opportunity to subtly let her body evolve toward her image without causing any serious shake-up in her belief system, and let her vibrations shift slowly without any major jolt in the bodies. Three months later she discovered that she had grown into the image and exactly matched it in attitude, hairstyle, and weight—and it was all accomplished unconsciously.

It's important to look at what kind of inner image you hold about yourself. When you create a new image of yourself, you're letting go of an idealized or outdated self-image, as well as getting rid of any extraneous people or objects that were attached to your picture. You compare yourself to this inner image unconsciously all the time, and if it doesn't accurately reflect your outer reality, you can never feel acceptable or happy with yourself.

By reshaping your image, you start cracking apart the belief that you are unworthy, and create space for something new and more positive to replace it.

EXERCISES

Changing Your Inner Image

It's important to do this exercise every few months in order to bring your image up to date.

1. Do the aura cleanout and create a present time field.

2. Close your eyes, and bring yourself into a quiet room inside your head. This is your private sacred space. Notice a picture of yourself on one wall. Examine it carefully.

3. What do you see in this picture?

   a. Is it of you right now, today? Not ten days ago, not ten weeks ago, not ten years ago—but *now*.

   b. How are you dressed? Stylish? Slovenly? In children's clothing? Ugly clothes? Do you like what you're wearing?

   c. What do you look like? Does it look exactly like you now? The same weight? What's your hairstyle? Are you too thin? Too fat?

d. Are you holding anything, or are there things in the picture besides you?

e. Are there other people in the picture, like your parents, spiritual teacher, etc.? If so, how do they look (gleeful, angry, hurt, judgmental)? What is their attitude toward you? Are they supportive, repressive, controlling?

f. When you look at the picture, notice how you *feel*—happy, unhappy, depressed, angry, contented, frustrated, etc.

g. For right now, accept yourself just as you are. Say this simple affirmation several times, "I completely accept myself and all my needs, problems, shortcomings, and desires." This particular affirmation accepts you as you are, and does not make judgments about you. (As you say these words, your mind may come up with comments, negative and positive. Just thank your mind for its comments and continue repeating the affirmation.)

4. Take your inner image off the wall and drop it into a handy vat of gold liquid (imagine one in the room with you). No matter how big the picture, the vat is large enough to contain it. Let it soak for a few moments.

5. Take the picture out of the vat. Does it look the same as before? Notice what's different. (There will be changes, no matter how subtle. If you don't see or sense them, don't worry. They have still occurred.)

6. Repeat the same affirmation (3-g).

7. Dispose of this picture in some way: Put it in a closet, blow it up, tear it up, break it into pieces, burn it, drop it in the ocean, etc.—whatever feels right to you.

8. With the help of your Higher Self, construct a picture of yourself that shows you as you wish to be in *three months*. If you're depressed, see yourself as somewhat happier; or if you're sick, see your health improving. If you're overweight, see yourself as a few pounds (5–10) lighter. Hang it on the wall.

9. If you don't know what to create, ask your Higher Self. It will provide the healthiest and most positive picture for you at this time.

10. Cover it with a gold ball of light, then let that gold light expand through your body and aura as well.

If you found yourself resisting the positive messages of this exercise, you may be reversed. See Chapter 7 for help with that problem.

The next exercise will help you remove the judgments you hold about your body. They become easier to remove when the image holding them in place gets torn down.

Cleaning Off Body Judgments

Doing this exercise is crucial. You may not realize how much you store within you other people's judgments about yourself, your mind, your body, or your self-image until you clean them out. They're like extra baggage you are lugging around. After doing this exercise, accepting who and what you see in the mirror is easier without the accretion of judgments and recriminations that have accumulated over the years.

1. Clean out your aura and put yourself into present time.

2. Put the beliefs you have about your body into a very large (person-sized) barrel full of gold liquid with a spigot at the bottom. The simplest method is to imagine putting a picture of yourself into the barrel, and letting it dissolve into the liquid.

3. Tap the barrel with the present time wand, so the liquid is in present time.

4. To remove beliefs about your body:

   a. Ask that all the beliefs that come from your family leave. Open the spigot and let that energy drain into the earth. (You may see it and all the other energies as particular colors; I have suggested colors, but you may have your own.) For this exercise, see family energy as red.

   b. Ask that all beliefs about yourself that you got from teachers and spiritual leaders be drained away. (See them as orange.)

   c. Pour out all the beliefs you absorbed from friends and relationships. (See them as dark green.)

   d. Drain away all the beliefs that came from television, advertising, and other outer sources. (See them as gray.)
      Whatever remains in the barrel belongs strictly to you. If you have very little liquid left, you have been strongly influenced by others. If there

is quite a bit, you have already managed to rid yourself of many outside influences.

Once you've drained away the foreign energies, you can shape your image as you would like it.

5. Ask the angels to fill the barrel with divine love, happiness, good feelings, and self-love. Imagine that each one of these is a sparkling lovely color.

6. Ask your Higher Self to add to the liquid acceptance of your body's shape and size as it is without judgments. You have created your "self mix." Stir.

7. When you've done all that, imagine climbing into the barrel to soak up these colored energies. Let them be absorbed into your body. For the first time, you are giving your body a new image of itself that is entirely different. You are perfect just the way you are!

8. When you're ready, you can climb out.

• • •

CHAPTER 7

CORRECTING REVERSAL

Some people are completely positive. Their affirmations and decrees work; their visualizations manifest. Their transformational processes come easily. Then there are people for whom things don't come so easily. You folks may find that whatever you consciously want, your body and mind create the opposite. That means if you try to lose weight, your body may either gain weight or hold onto what it has. Or if someone assures you, "You'll have no problem doing well," you not only disagree mentally, but you go on to prove them wrong by failing or sabotaging your own effort in some way. Or if you decide you're going to think positive, your mind promptly provides you with every possible reason to make you feel negative. You are in reversal.

How do you know you are reversed? Easy. If you do or think the *opposite* of what you're told, you are reversed. Reversal is not just a mental resistance or opposition. You simply cannot respond any other way.

Whenever you are in reversal, you live in a world of negativity. Reversal perpetuates a chosen status quo that you are living every day. This may be a one-issue reversal or it can overwhelm all the issues in your life.

A program has been set up in your mind so that you can only act on or accept negative ideas or beliefs. It has become hard-wired inside you, and it forces you to remain stalled in that negative place. Every time your mind activates this program (such as when someone says something positive), it reverses what you hear, and prevents you from accepting or creating anything positive. It's a self-fulfilling prophecy that only allows negation.

There are always precipitating reasons for creating the program (abuse of some kind), but once activated, it is extremely difficult to transform it into something positive. For example, when you feel you don't deserve love, all of your actions conspire to make yourself so unattractive (either physically or behaviorally) that you remain unloved. That provokes dislike or disgust toward yourself as well, which strengthens the self-negativity.

You can look back to your childhood for the creation of this internal negative program, to the rebellious Inner Child. She or he had already accepted their parents' assessment of them that they were not okay or lovable in some way (which made her or him feel worse). Nevertheless, they were determined to fight against those parental judgments and tyranny in the only way they knew how, which was to oppose them, either passively or actively. In spite of her or his rebelliousness, your Inner Child was fighting a losing battle because she or he was fighting from despair.

The Child in you is still fighting authority figures by repelling any ideas that argue against that old negativity. Even though you try to create positivity, you remain stuck in the negative.

No matter how many affirmations you say to yourself or how often, if you are reversed, their effect on you is minimal. (Since people who are not reversed have great success with affirmations, they can't understand why you don't.) It's like paddling upstream. You expend enormous energy fighting the current (the reversal); not only do you not move very far, but the experience is exhausting and discouraging.

Take women and their bodies. Generally, women have some degree of dissatisfaction and negative judgment about their bodies, whether it's about shape, weight, food needs, or food compulsions. Positive affirmations get turned around and simply reinforce that polarization, so that every positive statement you utter ("I am getting slimmer"), your mind counters with, "I will *not* lose weight! So there!"

Case Study: Lora tried to lose weight and went to a hypnotherapist to get some help. Even as she was being hypnotized, she changed every suggestion the hypnotherapist gave her to the opposite (from "you will lose weight" to "you will not lose weight") because she really wasn't ready yet.

Instead of a frontal assault on your reversal, which only provokes more resistance, you need to face the problem by *acknowledging and supporting who you are right now.* The more harshly you judge yourself, the more you feed that program. The only way to release that self-defeating program is to stop fighting against yourself by *accepting* yourself, starting with your parents' judgments about you. That means accepting that you are "not okay," at least in their eyes (which isn't true, but it's where you need to start).

Embracing the negative judgment disarms your inner combatants, unlike an all-out assault, which only stiffens resistance. Think of a Chinese finger puzzle (you stick your index fingers inside a woven tube). As you pull your fingers apart, the tube tightens so your fingers can't get free. By fighting it, you strengthen its hold on you even more. You can only release your fingers by pushing or relaxing into the tube. Reversal is a Chinese finger puzzle.

Arguing with the programmed negative belief gives it power. When you relax into yourself by finding and accepting whatever you hate the most about yourself, you can acknowledge that unloved part of yourself, and reclaim it as yours to love. Eventually, you can dismantle the negativity. Then, and only then, can you let it go. Reversal means you carry a cross that says, "I'm no good in some way." Being overweight is such a cross, especially if you hold negative judgments about your body.

Many women who were sexually abused as children create obese bodies to keep themselves protected. Their most personal space was invaded in a shocking, intimate way. By becoming very large and unattractive, they hope to keep their abuser at bay, so that he will find them too disgusting to touch (only sometimes does it work).

On the other hand, when you say, "I am a good and loving person, and I love myself however I am," or "My body is large because it's protecting me, and I love it for that," you begin to relax your grip on the resistance and move toward embracing yourself. (That's one important purpose of the fat rights movement—demanding acceptance of fat people, no matter how large—without any judgment, so they can feel good about themselves as they are.)

Earlier, I mentioned Lucy who hates her menopausal body, which feels completely unloved, and, therefore, only creates sickness for her. To heal, she needs to accept her body as it is, not as she wants it to be. That means recognizing how her body is helping her survive now before it will be willing to release any weight.

One of the hardest steps in your own inner work often can be accepting and embracing your reversed self because you perceive the symptoms or behaviors as repellent (like overeating or obesity). When you can finally understand what triggers those behaviors and why you still need them (that is, why your Inner Child is perpetuating them) you may feel more inclined to forgive yourself for your "flaws."

Once you see that these "flaws" have positive intentions, particularly trying to make you feel safe, no matter how grotesque, it becomes easier to accept and even love yourself. Dismantling the reversal can only come when you accept yourself; there is no other way.

Affirmations, even though they use positive statements, are a good first step. They activate your negative programming so you get an opportunity to bring into sharper focus the beliefs you really hold about yourself.

Another important step is changing the inner image you hold of yourself, with all of its concomitant negative judgments (see Chapter 6). Transforming that inner image brings your body image up to date. In doing so, you release a great deal of the self-hate and self-disgust wrapped up in that image, since the new image no longer gives them reinforcement. By bringing the inner image into present time, so that it reflects you as you are now, you detach the old judgments and energies that have stuck to it. That's a major step toward self-acceptance.

Until you love yourself as you are, you cannot release your reversal program and move on.

Next you can start forgiving yourself for your harsh self-judgments. Forgiveness is not an intellectual exercise. You must forgive yourself wholeheartedly—even if it takes repeating it over and over again until you really feel it (which you might not at first).

In the Image exercise in Chapter 6, you created an image of yourself in three months' time. If by the end of that period nothing changed or what you manifested was the opposite of your picture, a reversal program has kicked in. The exercise below (similar to the one in Chapter 6) is designed to counter your reversal by helping you accept your image as you are now.

EXERCISES

Bring Your Image into the Present

Accepting what you let yourself see in the mirror can be very healing. It's all part of the process of self-love.

1. Do the aura cleanout and create a present time field.

2. Close your eyes, and bring yourself into your private sacred space. Look at your picture on the wall. Notice how you like it. Has it changed from three months ago? Is it different from your real life image? If so, how?

3. Take this inner image off the wall and dispose of it in some way: Put it in a closet, blow it up, tear it up, break it into pieces, burn it, drop it in the ocean, etc.

4. Ask your Higher Self to help you construct a picture of yourself that reflects how you are right now. It will provide the healthiest and most positive picture for you at this time.

5. Hang it on the wall.

6. Cover it with a gold ball of light; then let that gold light expand through your body and aura as well.

7. Say the affirmation several times, "I completely accept myself and all my needs, problems, shortcomings, and desires." This affirmation accepts you as you are now, without judgments.

8. When you're finished, open your eyes.

Opposition

This exercise works very well with people who have negative beliefs about themselves. I will describe this exercise in terms of weight, but you can substitute any unwanted or troublesome emotions, or issues like feeling unworthy, ashamed, guilty, depressed, etc.

1. Close your eyes. Concentrate on your self-image, and enhance the feeling you wish to release. If you believe you are overweight, feel how wonderful it is to be that weight, how great it feels to eat all the food you want that keeps you at that weight *or makes you even larger.*

2. Think of the benefits to yourself to be at this weight. Yes, there are benefits! (Being heavy may make you feel safer, able to avoid unsafe feelings, emotions, relationships, commitments, or unwanted advances.)

3. If you cannot think of any benefits, ask your Higher Self to reveal the positive purpose for your behavior, attitude, or feeling.

4. Acknowledge your body for doing what it needed to keep you safe. ("Thank you, body, for keeping me safe from harm by being fat.")

5. If shame, guilt, anger, or other feelings arise as you do this visualization, acknowledge their presence and take a deep breath to release them. Imagine them as gray colors being expelled with each breath.

6. Fill yourself with the enjoyment of being large, letting it expand throughout your body, so you tingle and vibrate with satisfaction. See yourself eating food and enjoying the experience. (Even if most of your mind protests, say, "Thank you," and focus on the enjoyment of being that large size.)

7. Then imagine a large sunken bathtub filled with gold liquid. Climb into it. Sink all the way down, so the liquid covers your head (you can breathe in gold). Stay in there for a few minutes, and then climb out, leaving any emotions, feelings, energies, and weight that you're ready to release in the liquid.

8. Say the following forgiveness affirmations. Both of them will stir up a lot of feeling.

   a. I forgive my body for being the way it is.

   b. I forgive myself for being the way I am.

9. Repeat Step 7. This will begin to dissolve a lot of the emotion stirred up by saying those affirmations.

10. Repeat steps 4–7 again and again until you feel more comfortable with yourself or the negative feeling.

11. Do this imagery before meals, and every time a strong desire arises to eat something that would perpetuate your negative picture.

12. For other emotions, repeat these steps, except enhance the feeling of shame, depression, guilt, rage, etc.

Each time you do these steps, you will reduce that feeling in your body because you embrace the opposition, not fuel it. As you let the feelings get expressed, they can be rinsed away in the gold bath.

As a further incentive, as you do step 5, find a spot about one inch below each of your lower eyelids at the midpoint and tap that point twenty-five times. This is a meridian point that activates release of reversed or polar energies.*

• • •

---

* This step, adapted from Roger Callahan's book, *Why Do I Eat When I'm Not Hungry*, Avon Books, 1991, works for all feelings, not just food cravings.

CHAPTER 8

CHILDHOOD: THE EMOTIONS

Working with childhood issues means working with the emotional body. Do you hear someone inside you arguing, commenting, or criticizing you all the time? This voice is trying to keep you from processing feelings like anger, shame, abandonment, and love—which you hold in your emotional self. It knows that change—profound, real change—happens only with the complete involvement of your emotional self.

No matter how much you work on your issues, to clear them completely you must go back to their source. Think of a dandelion with its long taproot. Every time you chop off the plant, it comes back because the root still remains in the ground. Only when you remove the taproot completely will the dandelion not come back.

You need to transform your past at the deepest levels of your existence, digging out the root cause of the abuse, and tossing it on the compost heap of memory, so it will no longer survive with its trauma intact. That's the goal of changework, and it affects your emotional body profoundly.

Think of a trauma as a fist that continually pounds on you, leaving a huge purple bruise that never heals. The changework process effectively stops the fist from hitting you, so the bruise can finally fade away.

The Inner Child and Fear

The symbol of the emotional body is the Inner Child. She or he is wide-eyed and scared, living in a world shaped by fear of some kind—fear of harm, abandonment, shame, rage, or other emotions. Your Child's needs drive your adult behavior and shape your beliefs.

The level of fear indicates how strong the trauma is that the Inner Child has embedded in her or his body, and what obstacles must be overcome for healing to occur. By following your feelings down into yourself, you'll find your Inner Child. For her or him, your childhood traumas are not abstract memories; they are as alive now as when they occurred. Healing yourself means helping him or her break free of the spider web of the past so they can feel safe enough to let the traumas turn into memories.

As you evoke memories, the shame, fear, humiliation, rage, abandonment, and helplessness that you felt are activated. By transforming the memory, those painful feelings can finally dissipate.

For example, if you are afraid of authority figures because you had a rage-aholic father, releasing this childhood trauma from your emotional body means you no longer experience that same kind of overwhelming terror as an adult. The event will fade. You may still have twinges and memories for the rest of your life, but you can function without being governed by that fear.

Case Study: Fred was constantly humiliated by his tyrannical, perfectionist father. He could list one shame-filled experience after another, growing up. He was exquisitely aware of never achieving the perfection his father demanded. By healing those incidents, he released that crippling shame from his life.

Think of what happens when someone is angry with you. You can *feel* the anger like a fist punching you in the stomach, although you haven't been physically touched. Months or years later you still react to that memory, whether it is with fear, shame, or a corresponding anger. The other person's anger has been trapped in your body all that time. It must be removed for the feeling to be resolved. Either the present time wand or the golden comb will safely pull that energy out of your body.

Abuse that has embedded itself in your cells is harder to release; in that case you must re-create the memory in your inner world to release the emotional self's (Inner Child's) feelings, and heal the physical body's actual bruises, since those parts of you were the helpless victims on whom the abuse was inflicted.

In many cases, the same trauma comes up over and over again to be healed because the abuse (sexual, physical, emotional) continued over a long period of time. That means you may need to confront each child-hood event, until all of them are cleared.

Whenever you transform past events, several things happen:

- You release the stranglehold of that memory by turning traumas into simple memories and freeing up the trapped energy.

- You begin to reempower yourself because you can change the memory at will; no longer are you at the mercy of the past.

- You begin to forgive yourself for your actions, release your suppressed anger, and reclaim previously unacceptable emotions (that is, whatever was unacceptable in your family).

- You block off the old traumatic neuron pathways in your brain and create new loving and healing pathways.

- You create a space inside yourself to accept love and joy.

Before embarking on any inner work, you must remember that the person reliving this experience is your *Child*, not you. He or she made decisions about him or herself, their self-worth, and their lovability, based on being shamed, hurt, neglected, smothered, or abused. You may get angry at your child for his or her decisions, but remember, they chose survival, no matter what the consequences have been for you. You might want to take a moment to forgive your child for what he or she endured so that you could stay alive.

When you first confront your trauma, your Inner Child may not trust you enough to participate. But on a second or third attempt, you'll be more successful because he or she will have come to trust that you are serious about healing their traumas.

Finding a Memory

Before you begin, call on your Higher Self or a Guardian Angel to accompany you during this process. Inner resources like the Higher Self, Guardian Angel, and angels can help you negotiate the passage through your trauma with greater ease.

Ask your Higher Self to give you only as intense an experience as you can safely handle emotionally now *and later on*—so you won't become overwhelmed by whatever comes up. If you open yourself up without that precaution, you might crumble from the onslaught of the memory, not only during the changework, but in the weeks to follow.* I cannot emphasize enough that you rely on your Higher Self's wisdom. It knows how much emotional pain you can handle and how to protect you. In other words, don't get cocky; don't do your work without inner support!

Here are some ways to access memories:

- Recall a charged episode from your past, preferably childhood or early teenage years. Notice where you

---

* That's a major reason alcoholics and drug users stay addicted—to anesthetize their feelings. When they go into recovery, and the drugs finally leave their system (at about six months), the excruciating pain of the memories comes flowing back and can be almost unbearable. At that time they are most vulnerable to using their drug again, unless helped through the initial pain.

feel some kind of body sensation, for example, in the stomach, heart, genitals, throat, eyes. (There is no right or wrong feeling.) Some sensations may be emotional in tone (sad, angry, hurt) or physical (tightness, squeezing, fluttery feeling, heaviness, or stopped, shallow, or fast breathing).

- The absence of feeling, or numbness, is your body's mechanism for deadening your severe pain. Children of alcoholics are excellent at turning off their feelings. Notice where in your body you feel this deadness. If nothing still comes to mind, and that often happens when starting this kind of work, it simply means your body is trying to block you from feeling any deep emotional pain. It's a normal protective response.

- If you recall where you felt bodily pain when you did the alignment exercise in Chapter 5, those areas are ripe for changework. You can use them as avenues into your past. (Go back and do the exercise again to reacquaint yourself with these blocks, if necessary.)

- Finally, you can say the sentence, "I deserve love," twice. "I deserve love" carries an enormous emotional wallop. You'll hear at least one voice (or several) in your mind disagreeing with that statement, and you may have a concurrent physical or emotional reaction. Those mental voices are defending your belief system, so that whatever is not acceptable to that belief system (like deserving love) is immediately contradicted.

By this time, you're probably used to the mind's objections. Throughout the whole process, in fact, those mental voices may continue making comments, positive or negative. Acknowledge them by saying, "Thank you." Otherwise, they'll get more strident, like a persistent child tugging on your leg for attention. Once acknowledged, they will subside, or reduce their volume.

Seeing the Trauma

- Watch the story unfold on your inner television; don't become the Child. Observe her or him. Being an observer releases you from the grip of extremely painful emotions, so it becomes merely a television drama. If the incident is excruciating to watch, breathe slowly and deeply (at times like this, people either freeze or panic). You may want to trade it for another less-charged memory, at least for the first few times.

If you regress into the Child, with all the Child's emotions, try to dissociate yourself and remain an adult; by doing so, you will be able to access your adult resources.

Whenever you feel sucked into the story, you can do these things to separate or dissociate you from the past.

- Freeze the action. This gives you some perspective.

- Take some deep breaths.

- Open your eyes to reorient yourself into the present. Then go back into the memory.

- Ask your Higher Self to take over and keep you safe and on target.

A caveat: If you have difficulty with feeling anything, being the Child can help make the whole situation much more real, and the emotional release all the more powerful.

Releasing the Abuse

- As soon as you sense the parent start to abuse the child, invite your Higher Self and several angels to enter the scene with you and stop the action. Now, instead of the parent and child alone, there's a parent, a child, your Higher Self, angels, and you—the adult. Notice the parent's reaction; he or she *will* react to this audience.

  By stepping into the scene, you have created an as-yet-minor change in the brain pathways wired to this trauma, like deviating from your daily routine. As you continue to change the situation, your neurons will fire in new and different patterns, creating a new pathway. The ultimate goal is to create a memory of empowerment bathed in love.

  For the first time, the Child is no longer alone, defenseless or abandoned. She or he has been rescued from an abuser.

- Ask your Higher Self to hold and comfort your Inner Child. Actually holding a tangible soft object (stuffed animal or pillow) in your physical arms can trigger an enormous release in your emotional body (like anger or tears).

At this point your instinct might be to remove the Inner Child from the abusive situation rather than cuddle her. Don't. If you do, the abuse will remain stuck in *your* body. That's why another scenario must be created, with divine intervention.

- Call on the angels to "arrest" the abuser. No matter how threatening and deadly, he or she is no match for the power of an angel or two. Watch as two of them take him or her by the arms and escort them away from the child to a place where he or she can get re-education on how to be a good parent, or divine punishment if their "crimes" warrant it. (Let the Child decide what retribution is appropriate— and remember, your adult idea and your Child's idea may be wildly different.)

- As this occurs, your Child may feel one of two emotions—fury at the parent, terror at being abandoned, or both at the same time. Kids normally don't want to hurt their parents or get rid of them, no matter how abusive they've been, since the kids live in constant dread of being abandoned. Let your Higher Self reassure your Child that she or he is no longer alone, that they are protected by the Higher Self and the angels, and that no one will hurt them.

- Watch while the angels remove the pain of the experience from your body. Imagine them opening a closet within you and allowing all of the pain and emotions trapped in the memory to fall into a hole in the ground, removed from your space forever.

Then let them spread divine approval and love over the child (you can visualize it like a sparkly, golden fog, or just a sparkly sensation). *You don't have to do any work or even imagine it; it just happens.* Allow it to fill you as well. Flooding the whole scene with this divine energy absorbs all the old toxic energies from the trauma and leaves space for joy and love. Whether or not you truly want to give all the pain away (for holding on to your pain is often very important), letting divine love flow through you alters your brain, chips away at your mind's belief system, releases the trauma from your emotional body, and frees up your energy.

Anger

During this process, (or perhaps days or weeks later) your Child (and you, the adult) will start feeling rage. Let your Child kick, yell, pound a pillow (pretending it's the parent) until they are done. Children have stuffed a lot of fury down inside themselves. The more traumatized the child, the greater the suppressed rage that needs to be expressed (no matter what you would like).

Sexually abused children were betrayed on two levels—first, physically (incest is a universal taboo); and second, emotionally—because the parent both manipulated the child into believing he or she was the cause of the incest, and violated the parental role. The Child grows up not trusting her or his feelings of love, and filled with enormous rage.

The Inner Child must be allowed to express her or his feelings, no matter what they are. Your disapproval of this justifiable anger is just as destructive as your parents' abuse, even though you may cringe at letting your Child express anger. No matter. Your adult reason and civility have no reality for the Child. She or he must let their primal emotions out, so they can be released from you.

Anger has its place. Many of us don't like to see or experience it because it is intense energy (and actually pretty high, vibrationally). Your Child needs not only to express it, but to feel accepted and loved while doing so. If you cannot accept their anger, your Higher Self and the angels can. Allow the gold fog of divine love to flow into that Child so that she or he can bathe in its vast total acceptance, and experience its enormous healing. Meanwhile, if you can send your judgment about anger to the Godhead while watching your Child emote, you will release that judgment.

Release

During much of the changework process, you may have cried, yelled, or even remained silent. The more you feel, the stronger your release. If you treated the process as an intellectual exercise and experienced little emotion, even with the angelic love, merely doing it lets your body know that you are open to change—and angelic love will work on you at a subtle level. After a while as you continue your changework, the emotions will begin to pour out because your Child will feel safe enough to let out her or his long-suppressed feelings.

Reliving an event not only releases it in both the physical and emotional bodies, it raises your vibration because energy has been freed from the trauma and

99

cleaned off. Your Child certainly feels different (you can't help it, feeling divine love changes you, whether you believe it or not). *You* feel different.

Once the emotional abscess has been drained, you have created a space to fill up with new life and vitality. Take a moment now to breathe in the gold angelic fog and let it fill up all those places inside you that no longer contain those traumatic toxins. Thank your Higher Self (or Guardian Angel) for helping and guiding the process.

EXERCISE

Releasing a Childhood Trauma

1. Find a quiet place to do this work. You don't want to be disturbed. Put on soft music, if you wish. Have a pillow and stuffed animal handy. Do the aura cleanout and present time field.

2. Call in your Higher Self or Guardian Angel.

3. Choose a memory. (Don't pick something deeply traumatic like sexual abuse the first time, just an incident that gives you an uncomfortable buzz.) If you don't have one readily available you can do one of the following:

   a. Say, "I deserve love," twice. It will cause a reaction inside you. Then ask your Higher Self to bring up the memory of the first time you experienced that feeling in your childhood.

b. Imagine there's a large suitcase, and inside that suitcase are your painful memories. Reach inside and pull one out.

c. Repeat the alignment exercise on page 60.

4. Watch the event unfold until the abuse starts.

5. Call in the angels.

6. Step into the scene as the adult with the angels and your Higher Self.

7. Give the Inner Child to your Higher Self. Hold the stuffed animal or another pillow and rock your Child.

8. Ask the angels to remove the parent for divine re-education. If the Child wants to hit and scream at the parent, pound on the pillow until he feels complete or drained of the rage.

9. Let angelic love fill the room (as the gold fog). Bathe in its essence of pure and total acceptance.

10. When you're finished, open your eyes.

You might notice nothing at the moment, but later on you may have an emotional reaction or a sense of release. These inner changes take time to work through, depending on the extent of your blocks. You will be getting all kinds of shifts for them throughout the next few weeks, like the pieces of an intricate hand puzzle clicking into alignment. The more work you do during this time, the more opportunity for letting go of more blocks. The effect is cumulative.

CHAPTER 9

WHO YOU
~~ATTRACT~~

Who is out there for you? What kind of person do you attract?

Before you started down your path of self-evolution, you had absorbed the patterns, beliefs, and ideas that attracted you to a certain type of partner or lover based on the primary adult relationship you watched as you grew up—that of your parents. This unconscious but entirely influential program has remained with you as an adult, governing your choice of partner. It says, "I need somebody who I can be codependent with," or "I need somebody who I can ignore but who will take care of my needs." "And, by the way, since my mother/father drank, I want to attract an alcoholic or other kind of addict as well."

Even though your conscious mind may try to choose differently, the relationship you form with your lover fulfills your emotional needs based on your parents' relationship, no matter what you want. It also guarantees that you will create the same set of circumstances you had as a child, except that now you're an adult. This is a self-fulfilling prophecy.

> **Case Study:** Nina says all she has to do is go to a party, and the only man who looks cute will turn out to be the only addict at the party—just like her father. (This is a frighteningly common occurrence for many of us.)

Did you have a childhood with a violent father and compliant mother? Unluckily, you're apt to be either violent and marry someone who's compliant, or be compliant with a violent or rageful marriage partner. Either you act like your parents, or the exact opposite of them. In that case, you haven't broken free of the pattern; you're just polarized, with the same internal family dynamics flipped inside out.

What makes this whole process even crueler is that each time you get involved with a new partner, for about four to six months you're in paradise because you believe you've found your perfect lover. This time your lover is not like your parent. Then the rosy glasses come away from your eyes, you can see your partner more clearly—and the honeymoon's over. You find that you have created the same relationship all over again.

You then wonder to yourself whether you're in love with this person any more, but since you're lying next to him/her, you two are either going to accept each other's flaws and make this relationship work, or you are going to split up. Should you finally move on to the next relationship, you repeat the whole process with the same result. Over and over again.

You may not realize that your choice of partner is completely predictable—as well as the progress of your relationship. Afterward, you say to your friends in dismay, "How could I have gotten involved with that person?" They can only sigh. Then when you go and do it again with the same kind of person, they go, "Yuck! Not again!" (They're no better because they do the same thing as well. It's just easier to recognize when someone else makes mistakes, not yourself.)

Later on, you shake your head, wondering, "Why do I keep attracting these same people? What is wrong with me?" Enough pop psychology books have been written about bad relationships to provide answers to this question. Ultimately, it comes down to, "You attract what you know" (that means parents), and this attraction is closely attached to your childhood survival mechanisms.

Your mental screens filter out candidates according to criteria that include a strong similarity (or opposition) to one of your parents if one or both were addicted.

Every time you feel a pull toward someone, you are being activated by old patterns, primarily from your first chakra (survival), even though your second chakra (sex) may trigger the initial attraction and contact. When you say, "My heart is choosing this person," it rarely does. Your first chakra and your internal programming are really making the choice to attract what you know.

It's rare that you choose a lover from your heart or your head, although it may feel that way. You can consciously state your preference for one kind of person, but an unconscious part inside you (the Inner Child) has a different set of criteria for its choice—primarily involving personal safety.

All of your relationships have a survival quality to them. As a child you knew you could only survive by acting in a certain way to get your needs met (whether it was love or attention) or to avoid pain or shame. Now as an adult, struggling to make adult choices, you're still governed by your child's need for safety, and that plays the critical role in your choice of lover/partner.

A familiar relationship, healthy or not, makes you feel safer because you know how to function in that environment. That means you're more apt to remain in an abusive relationship than leave because of its familiarity, and you know what's expected of you—no matter how painful it may be (unless you've done some serious work on changing your patterns)—it's "the devil you know...."

You don't have to take on all the responsibility for your relationship, however; you're only half of the problem. If you have a certain attraction program, your partner has a similar one, with similar survival criteria. Both of you are equally responsible for choosing each other.

Reprogramming Yourself

The famous Sufi story of the six blind men and the elephant illustrates this point beautifully: Each man touched a different part of the elephant (tail, tusk, leg, trunk, ear, body), so they extrapolated what the elephant looked like from how that part had felt. Their inner images were therefore imperfect because no one saw the whole beast.

You are like those men, seeing only one or two perspectives. By removing and releasing screens and the negative energies and patterns from your space, you can see a much more multi-dimensional picture of your world (whereas before you saw just one piece of it); therefore, you can perceive old messages or old screens with new and greater clarity.

It's like replacing a small window with a picture window. Once the vista has gotten larger, unless you put the small window back you simply can't have the narrow view you did before. When you see the whole elephant through your enlarged window, you can correct your erroneous perception.

As you chip away, bit by bit, at your old patterns and beliefs, and reclaim your energy, you'll find yourself making new choices about what kind of people you want in your life—as friends, and more particularly, as lovers.

When that begins to happen, the people around you will do everything they can to disrupt the process, including forcing you back into your prior dysfunctional behavior.

That will present you with a choice: Should you take care of them—or you? Some available options include the following: 1) You choose to continue healing, and they accept the new you and change themselves; or 2) you accede to their pressure and revert to your old behavior; or 3) you split up.

Your relationship at the beginning of the change process may fracture when you decide not to tolerate dysfunctional interactions any longer. As you start dismantling your inner structure, ideally those inner patterns that attracted you to your partner disappear, so there is something else to support your relationship. (Couples counseling is strongly recommended here.)

As you proceed along your healing path, your partner may choose to change as well, so you both may grow. Unfortunately, in many instances, the differences between you two become insurmountable and you may split up. Even if you do revert to old behaviors, you're apt to split up sooner or later because it's very difficult to turn back into your old self. Then you're left looking for a new relationship, hoping to create something different the next time.

That's why women in their forties and fifties are going wild. Once they realized they deserved meaningful, mutually caring, and equal relationships, they ditched their husbands, who were their age or older, because the men were rigid and hidebound, refusing to change and transform (although a small number of men in their forties and fifties have begun to work on themselves). These women have decided that, though they dearly want another relationship, they'd rather create their own women's support system than remain with abusive, unsupportive partners.

As long as you continue to work on yourself, your subsequent relationship will be different because you won't fall back automatically on old patterns and beliefs.

Whenever you create a Present Time Field and clean out your aura (ideally, every day), whatever has been stirred up inside you gets removed. That means whenever an old screen is suddenly activated, such as the one that says you can only be involved with certain types of people, you can reduce its influence by releasing its energy so that eventually it is removed.

One way to do that is by asking yourself, "What do I get out of attracting this kind of person?" Asking that question allows you to examine your motives—which usually have safety as a basis. When you can turn your attention to the price you paid for the partner you chose, you can begin to make other choices. By altering any part of your past, you start the process.

Healing your childhood traumas breaks your tangled connection with the abuser, whether it was your mother or father.

Case Study: Marcy came to me to break her smoking habit. She was raised in a rural household by parents who were religious fanatics. She received no love from either of them. The only people who gave her any love (such as it was) were a bunch of teenagers, and they smoked. Through Inner Child work, she learned that she wouldn't stop smoking because smoking she equated with love.

Marcy's idea of love was wired into a belief that said, "Only smokers can love me." When she disconnected the belief that cigarettes equalled love, we could then deal with her addiction.

This is where the angelic presence is very helpful. Angels are filled with an enormous, inexhaustible source of love, and they're glad to funnel it into you. Angels love your Inner Child without judgment or conditions. Their love is unconditional, ever-flowing, and inexhaustible. All you have to do is accept it. Even though the adult may have trouble doing that, your Child won't—not from an angel. Children trust angels.

You learned as a child that you could have love with certain restrictions ("I can have love when it's given to me with a slap on the side of the head, or when I'm criticized, or when my husband (parent) approves, or when I perform the right role"), so you don't believe that you deserve love. Besides, there is only a finite (and small) amount of love in the world. Both of those beliefs are *simply not true.* If you are feeling unloved and unworthy, or if you have been programmed not to accept love, it's very difficult to perceive it.

Releasing the Program

Taking the steps required to change means replacing the attraction program, which is hardwired inside your brain. The energy circuits of the lower chakras are gummed up by old programming about love. (The following chart illustrates that programming.)

1st Chakra:	Love	=	Survival
2nd Chakra:	Love	=	Sex
3rd Chakra:	Love	=	Power/manipulation
4th Chakra:	Love	=	With conditions

Those equations must be reformulated before bringing new, more healing beliefs into you, so you need to reconfigure your chakras to attract a new vibration.

Your first chakra, at the tailbone, governs survival of all kinds. Since anything you do may affect your physical survival, your first chakra is always activated, even if only at a very low level. That means anything having to do with love is assessed according to how safe you will be. By clearing the program that attracts a partner based on safety needs (that is, its familiarity—this is "the devil you know" concept), you don't have to follow those old patterns any longer.

Your second chakra (three inches above your groin) governs sexuality. Stuck in here is the sexual energy that equates love with sex (for example, women as sex objects, not sex partners). That kind of demeaning energy needs to be eliminated. That doesn't mean getting rid of *sexuality* or the joy of sex, just the program that dehumanizes or debases your partner.

The energies to be removed from your third chakra at your solar plexus are power over others and manipulation. Power is fine, but not when used to control or dominate. Control can either be naked (through emotions like anger) or covert (through manipulation as in playing the victim or using guilt).

Finally, your fourth chakra is your heart. Very early on you learned that love is conditional, and unless you acted a certain way, you were unworthy of it. These two very destructive messages need to be removed from your heart chakra and replaced by the message that love is inexhaustible and flowing; and you *always* deserve it.

To do that, you need to visit each chakra, and change or remove the "attraction template" created by you many years ago. I visualize it as a switchboard you see in old movies, where the operator plugs the cord from the incoming call into the socket for the person receiving the call.

Another similar image is a player piano. The roll is already prepunched so the piano can only play set keys—and nothing else.

It is exactly the same with your attraction template. It doesn't matter what you think you want; you can't change the program. It's already been set up to allow in only somebody who matches that prearranged configuration (unless you've done a lot of work on yourself).

It's time to change or retire this template by first unplugging all the cords and wires hooked into your template so you can release all the survival links you have with all of your partners, and with your parents. You may suddenly feel some strange and even uncomfortable feelings, like abandonment or fear. Don't worry; it takes some time to get used to the idea that you are no longer controlled by other people's programs.

If you feel you want to plug them back in after you do the exercise, you will be able if you want to—but, frankly, once they're gone, it's far healthier for you to keep them out. The only place you should have any connecting cords is in your heart chakra. Any other cords are intrusive and off-balancing.

The next step is to actually remove the template from your first chakra, clean it off, and bring it into present time. Once you have seen the condition it is in, you can choose to rewire it, or create another one altogether. It depends on the condition of your old template after it has been cleaned.

Should you choose to retain your old template, it simply means you are content to make changes at a more deliberate pace. If it is unusable, you've been ready to dispose of it for a long time, but didn't have the knowledge or resources to get rid of it.

If you create a brand-new template, you are, in effect, creating something brand-new inside yourself, which will trigger all sorts of changes in your attitude. You're ready for more rapid change.

When you rewire your template (old or new), you let go of old limiting programs. Your life and your connection with your partner *will* shift because the underpinnings of your old relationship no longer exist. You can create new ones that reflect the new improved you. That's proof that your changework is making a difference.

EXERCISE

Rewiring Your Attraction Template

1. Put on some meditation music. Get yourself comfortable. Do the cleanout exercises and get the present time wand (in Chapter 4). Close your eyes, and call in your Higher Self.

2. You are going to visit your first chakra, which is at the base of your spine (your tailbone). This chakra is associated with survival and is directly linked to your reptilian brain (medulla). You will not see the actual physical tailbone but rather the emotional body tailbone. From the center of your head, step onto an escalator and let it carry you and your Higher Self down to the tailbone.

3. Step off the escalator and look around. Whatever you see in your chakra is symbolic. If you con't see anything, you might sense or hear something. Ask your Higher Self to show you the Attraction Template that forces you to choose the same old partner.

4. Reach out and unplug any cords attached to that template. If you do not see them, imagine that you are unplugging them anyway. Say to yourself, "I am pulling all the cords out of the template and sending them back to whomever they belong (parents, lover, friends)." You can imagine them zipping away like a vacuum's retractable cord.

5. Tap the template with your present time wand to bring it into present time. (I guarantee you, this template is about as far from present time as you are

from the moon.) You might notice an instant change, either in the image or in your tailbone. Then pry it off the wall. If you can't do it easily by yourself, call on your Higher Self or the angels for help.

6. Drop it into a convenient vat of gold liquid to soak. If there are other pieces of hardware in your chakra that kept your template bolted to the wall, remove them as well and throw them into the vat; they belong to your old way of thinking. If you can't remove the template, pour gold liquid over it. Then it will come off more easily.

7. This template is linked to the medulla by a large cable. You may see or simply sense the cable. Ask your Higher Self to send a gold ball of light through the top of your head to fill the medulla. Let the light flow down the cable to your first chakra. As it covers the cable, it dissolves any old programming attached to it.

8. Detach the cable from your medulla and your first chakra, and throw it into the gold vat for recycling.

9. Take the template out of the vat. Observe its condition. If it is tenuous, thin, broken, torn, cracked, holey, or otherwise useless, throw it back into the vat for recycling.

10. Ask your Higher Self to create a new template that reflects the new You.

11. If your old template looks pretty good after its bath, you can keep it—at least for now. Ask your Higher Self to make sure it has more holes (options) and put them into the template if that's required.

12. Hang the template (old or new) on the wall with new attachments provided by your Higher Self.

13. Ask your Higher Self to run a new golden cord from your medulla down to the template. Since the first chakra governs survival, it does need to be hooked into the brain's survival mechanism, but just not in the old constrictive way.

14. Ask the angels to flood the first chakra, the cord, and the medulla with love and healing. Your first chakra has been on the front line of survival for so long, it doesn't need to protect you so vigorously. You have other resources now.

15. When you're finished, open your eyes.

When you're ready to work on the other chakras, repeat the exercise for your second, third, and fourth chakras. You do not need to do steps 6, 7, and 12.

In practical terms, doing this exercise means that you are no longer wired for your old relationships. That doesn't mean that you instantly start attracting someone different. After all, you still have the programming in other places—like your mental body's screens, your aura, and your emotional body, But doing this work means you might have a harder time clinging to those beliefs and patterns because the root of the need is no longer there. You can begin to make other less damaging choices for your life.

You may also use this exercise for other issues, such as success, poverty, self-esteem, or fear.

• • •

CHAPTER 10

THE FROZEN MOMENT

If you could imagine your life as a road down which you have been journeying, what would it look like? Take a moment now to close your eyes and visualize your road and its surroundings. You might find yourself teetering on a twisted, steep footpath on the side of a craggy mountain, or strolling down a pleasant garden lane, or perhaps trudging through a parched desert landscape. What is your terrain like? How straight is your road? What's coming up ahead? Now turn around and see what you survived. Whatever images you see of your road symbolize the kind of life you've chosen to live.

Yet if you could soar above your road and track it all the way back to its origin, you'd notice how sometimes your road took strange jogs, or there were barriers or huge craters or fissures that forced you to move in another direction altogether. Such places are pivot points—events that caused massive and profound changes in your life. Sometimes they are good, while often they indicate disasters that produced devastating consequences leaving you an emotional and psychic wreck. I call these jolts "frozen moments."

Examples of such devastating pivotal moments might be sexual abuse, rape, the death of someone close to you, divorce, major illness, war, or other calamities or disasters. Today, we label the psychological effects of these crises as post-traumatic stress, and we know they color and control everything we do, even years after the event. Every one of us probably can recall at least one or two pivotal moments that totally reshaped our lives and sent us spinning off on a new direction. The incredible shock of these serious blows to our system may cause us to change our nature in some profound way.

Case Study: When Louisa was a sophomore in college, she was date raped—and it shattered her life. She had planned on pursuing singing as a career until the rape. After that, she was convinced that she was a "bad girl" (for going out on that date against her parents' wishes), and as punishment, she not only got raped, but she found she could no longer perform in public. She became a business major, and she withdrew into herself, becoming quiet and self-effacing— and most importantly, she always blamed herself for causing the rape. Twenty years later she was deeply depressed, very unhappy about her job, miserable in her marriage, and wishing she were dead.

When I asked Louisa to tell me the most significant moment of her life—she immediately mentioned the rape, for she had never escaped its effects. Louisa had become frozen in time. The rape had so overwhelmed her psyche that everything subsequently was a direct result of it. It had become the single defining moment of her life.

The result of such a frozen moment is that we either stop growing and stunt our selves, or grow in a different, less healthy way, which may include addiction, to escape from the memory and the pain. A frozen moment cuts us off from our full potential in a markedly dramatic way. Because of the rape, Louisa literally choked off her gift of song, believing she was unworthy of it. When she picked up the pieces of her life, she created a functional adulthood, choosing a career as a businesswoman because it was safe, but her joy and her life force were blocked off and inaccessible.

People can experience frozen moments from local, national, or international events. Where were you when President Kennedy was shot? That one moment may not have changed the course of American history, but it certainly changed the American psyche. It has scarred us all.

A far more devastating frozen moment for Americans is the Vietnam War. Every one of our values was tested, rejected, or altered because of that conflict—and many people found their lives markedly and profoundly changed. The Vietnam War remains an open wound that still obsesses us, decades after its end. As a country, we have not released the trauma of that time; and many individuals who served there still suffer severe post-traumatic stress. Even the people who didn't serve lost their innocence during those turbulent 60s.

Case Study Rose Ann and her brother Roy had an argument; then he went swimming and drowned. She never forgave herself for having parted from Roy in anger, or that their father was terribly upset that his only son died. She never recovered her self-esteem and it haunts her to this day.

How can you recognize a frozen moment? It has several characteristics:

- It changed your life in some serious way, so that your life veered off in a direction far different from the one you planned. A good example is of Vietnam veterans, many of whom are still trapped in the jungle, whether as street people or in wilderness areas in various parts of the country.

- It controls your life, whether or not you speak of it, or even recall it. Vietnam veterans breathe it every moment of their lives. Many sexual abuse victims who have suppressed memories of their abuse have an underlying feeling that "something is wrong" that they can't put a finger on. The devastating event has become an obsession, whether or not it is in their consciousness.

- It is intensely alive in the present moment. If the frozen moment is not personally shameful (like sexual abuse), you bring it up in conversation (like a death, divorce, catastrophe, etc.), over and over again, like a mantra. Your hope is that by talking about it a lot you will either come to terms with it, or diminish its impact. (This is a belief in many kinds of counseling—that talking about something enough will reduce its power.) Instead, you relive it over and over and over.

- You measure yourself according to the event. "If X hadn't happened, I would have been..." or "If X hadn't happened, I could have done..." or "Since X happened, I can never be/do/have Y because I'm no good/I'm shameful/I'm to blame." Messages like that diminish you, as well as keep you stuck.

- You are no longer able to deal with things that you could handle before the event—even years later that emotional ability is still missing. It's like having a stroke and regaining only partial use of a limb—you cope, but not nearly as well as before.

A frozen moment prevents you from living up to your potential; for your own psychological and spiritual healing, it must be released from your self. We all experience enormously powerful events, but how we deal with them determines our future.

Until recently, people suffered from their experiences in silence. Now that we know much more about the effects of grief, date rape, incest, and molestation, therapists and support groups can help people work through their pain and resolve the trauma. You no longer have to suffer post-traumatic stress forever alone. Louisa began attending a rape support group, as well as continuing her therapy, and between these two methods, she completely transformed herself. (One of the keys to her healing was accepting that she was not to blame for the rape. Once she internalized that message, she could stop punishing herself.)

In determining how your frozen moment(s) has affected your life, it is important to consider the following questions. (Do not worry if you cannot come up with answers at first, particularly for something like sexual abuse. You have suppressed those memories for your own survival.)

- What incident(s) in your life do you talk about over and over again? Ask friends for help if you are not sure. They'll know!

- What did you give up after you experienced your frozen moment? It may be a career, family, a relationship, a belief system, trust in self/others/God.

- What "bitter lesson" did you learn from the experience? Usually, it's something for which you judge yourself harshly—like Louisa blaming herself for her rape—or if you blame yourself for being molested as a child by an adult who told you that your behavior or looks caused that person to molest you.

- What has been the price of your loss? In other words, what would your life have been like if that had not occurred? Maybe it happened early enough in your life that you don't know; but most of the time you have a sense of how you'd have lived.

- Are you willing to resolve your frozen moment? (You'd be surprised how many people are not willing because it keeps them from having to take responsibility for changing their lives.)

When you decide to deal with the frozen moment and its impact on your life, you may need to pry open a part of yourself that has been sealed off for years, and access the emotions, feelings, and abilities you cut off. That can be terrifying, but if you look at the process from the perspective of healing your pain, you can release the trauma and reclaim lost parts of yourself.

Once Louisa realized that she was not to blame for the rape, she began to take steps to heal her shame and trauma, like going to a rape crisis group, and then seeking out people who gave her approval rather than disparagement and judgment (as had her husband and mother). Eventually, she began to perform in amateur theatricals.

Doing this work means releasing lots of anger and allowing self-forgiveness. It requires you to go back and reclaim that lost part of yourself. That means removing the abuser from your energy field and reformulating the event (see Chapter 8).

Your frozen moment is stuck in the past. This exercise will give you an idea of how ready you are to deal with your frozen moment by "seeing" the box that holds the event's energy. To be able to see it clearly, and not be overwhelmed by its memories, it needs to be in present time.

Think of the mountain and the molehill. The longer you've endured it, the more of your energy it has trapped, so that even looking at the frozen moment can be daunting. Cleaning it off with the present time wand will help immensely. Then you will have the opportunity to open the box and remove as much energy as you want. The key, of course, is not just whether you are able to take out any energy—but whether you can even open the box. Most people cannot take anything out of the box the first time they open it. Just seeing the box in present time can trigger an enormous emotional reaction. This is the first time that you are actually confronting a shattering experience—no matter how mildly.

EXERCISE

The Frozen Memory Box

1. Close your eyes and do your cleanout. Hold on to the present time wand; you'll need it for this exercise.

2. Call in your Higher Self and at least one angel.

3. Imagine a red box. That is your frozen moment. Your box may be of any size, shape, texture, material, or color.

4. Observe the box. How do you feel just looking at the box? Are you angry? Sad? Happy? Terrified?

5. Take a few deep breaths, and ask the angels to bathe you and the box in sparkling gold love energy.

6. Tap the box with the present time wand.

7. If you are able, open the box. Inside is all of the energy from that experience that has been locked away.

8. If you don't feel capable of opening the box yourself, but you DO want it opened, ask your Higher Self to do it for you. Notice how you feel as the box is opened.

9. Take a gold dipper. Reach in and scoop out some of your locked-away essence. Take out as much energy as you are able to reclaim. What is it like to do that?

10. Look at what's inside the dipper. Is it liquid or an object? Tap it with the present time wand.

11. If it's liquid, pour it over your head and let it be absorbed into you.

12. If you see an object, put it into your heart.

13. You probably will feel some kind of emotion—perhaps strongly, perhaps not. This is the first step toward reclaiming who you were.

To further continue healing your frozen moment, I suggest three avenues to pursue:

- Repeat this exercise and take more of your essence back.

- Find a support group that can be there for you.

- Get therapy.

The combination of a trained professional and a loving supportive group with similar issues is quite powerful. Combined with this exercise, they will help you reclaim the wonderful person you were before you froze.

CHAPTER 11

LIFESTREAM: A RIVER

It's easy to imagine life as a timeline. You are born, you grow up, you grow old, and finally you die. Time appears to be linear, with a past, present, and future. In the last chapter, I talked about life as a road. This time the metaphor is a river which I call the lifestream.

A river flows downhill, seeking the path of least resistance until it reaches the sea. When the river approaches its mouth, if the land is flat, it may become a delta, breaking into rivulets and streams that flow in their own meandering course to the sea. The Nile delta is the most famous example.

Imagine your lifestream as a river flowing out of the Godhead, which is the source of your life energy, as Lake Victoria is one source of the Nile. When you are born, an enormous life force, which you can call "endless possibility," pours out of the Godhead—energy that is available for you in whatever way you wish to use it. Everything is possible or attainable—until you start making choices.

An infant makes every single sound in the world when he's first gurgling and cooing. As he listens to the sounds around him, he eliminates those sounds that he doesn't hear and mimics the ones he does. When he starts speaking, even just "meaningless" syllables, he speaks in the intonation of the language he hears. If his parents are Chinese, he uses tonality; if Xhosa, clicks. He chooses those particular sounds in order to be understood, so that when he speaks, he makes only those sounds from the language he hears.

That is very similar to what happens emotionally with your Inner Child. As you proceed down your lifestream, you make choices to break off or eliminate those parts of yourself that will hinder your receiving your allotted supply of love and sustenance. If you learn that yelling and screaming will cause you to be ignored or abused in some fashion, you may cut that angry/ frustrated part of yourself off and become compliant, in order to get love. None of these decisions are conscious, but they were made in the earliest stages of your life.

When that happens, you deny the existence of a part of yourself. That causes your lifestream to split, creating a tributary that siphons away the part of you that is "boisterous and loud." Even though you continue on with your life, you've become diminished to some degree. When you make the next decision to split off a part of yourself because of a shame or guilt situation, for example, you discard more pieces of yourself. Every emotional decision that forces you to cut off parts of yourself diminishes you. The belief system that shackles your mind cuts off more pieces of your lifestream.

As you can imagine, at present, your lifestream is nowhere near as strong and powerful as when you were born. If you lose too much of your energy, you become prey to sickness. When you reclaim yourself and your energy through changework, you begin to recognize how much energy you have lost.

Going Back

Since this book focuses on self-change, working on your lifestream can help you regain your energy by changing not just the past, but the future, as well. Lifestream work does not change a *memory* (as other techniques do), but the *energy* around the issue itself.

Lifestream work involves reshaping your inner landscape by going back to the points where the river branched off, healing the split, and reclaiming that lost energy. If you were surveying your river from an overhead perspective, your river would look like a root system, with a multitude of thick or thin branches split off from the central stalk (see illustration, page 134).

Each fork or branch is a point at which you lost some of your lifestream. If you dip your feet into the stream above any fork, you can sense what it felt like before you gave up that part of yourself. As you proceed farther back, your lifestream energy feels much different from your energy today. It's easy to realize how diminished your lifestream is because so much of it has been drained away by memories and feelings. Your goal is to blend all of those streams back into the main lifestream so their energy will be available to you again.

129

Let's use shame as an example. Shame goes back to the earliest days of toddlerhood, so it is one of the earliest splits. Someone's disapproval or judgment provoked shame, which caused you to split off a part of yourself. Disapproval directed at you in other situations creates more branched-off shame forks, so that even more of your energy gets diverted.

In reconnecting the branches, it seems really attractive to travel back to the original split, but it's like childhood changework; you have to go back in stages; otherwise the disruption to your psyche and your body can be devastating. Going back to that primordial branch the first time is unwise and far too difficult, and would cause an enormous emotional upheaval inside you. Healing needs to proceed step by step to allow your bodies (all of them) to adjust to the changes.

You need first to reclaim your life force from a fairly recent time when you experienced shame. This provides you with more energy and more skill as you move back up the stream, healing earlier events.

When you reach a fork in the river, you will find some kind of object or symbol in the lifestream of the trigger that caused the split. That symbolic object belongs to something or someone outside of you. Even though you made the split, you would not have done so without an impetus from without (disapproval, shaming, anger, abandonment). It might be a ball of energy or objects obstructing the stream, like rocks, stones, logs, statues. The object, which appears different from the surroundings and out of place, contains energy of the situation that precipitated the split. It needs to be removed. Otherwise, it will hamper you from healing the split completely.

You rarely find actual people at the forks, only their energy in some symbolic form. Now, even though both you and they may have long since forgotten about the incident or the connection, that symbol's presence still keeps your energy unavailable to you.

You must remove those objects—otherwise nothing can be done to heal the diverted stream. You can pour gold acid onto them (harmless to you and your environment, but it melts the alien objects), invite the earth to swallow them up, or ask angels to remove them. Any of these methods releases them from your space permanently.

Once the obstruction is removed, it becomes much easier to block the flow of life energy to the branch, and then eliminate the fork itself. For this step, you can call in your Higher Self for help. There are many images you can use. Here are a few suggestions:

- Ask a bunch of beavers to create a dam.

- Use bulldozers to create a wide earthen dam.

- Dynamite the branch so it creates a landfill.

- Cause a landslide.

- Bring in some angels to create a magical barrier.

- Have the Starship Enterprise blast in a dam using its phaser.

Get Creative

Once you block off the split, that energy no longer gets leached away from you. Not only do you remove the alien energy, you recover a piece of yourself that you lost, and you have altered your lifestream energy.

> **Case Study:** Florence visualized herself taking a motorboat back to a branch that made her feel inadequate and helpless. There, she discovered a huge, howling stone statue of a close friend who had ridiculed her. Its sound cut right through her heart, so that she could barely think clearly. Her Higher Self stepped in and arranged to have the statue removed by angels. When that happened, she felt a much greater lightness in her heart. Then she called in beavers to construct a dam to block off that fork. Afterward, she recognized that this was the first step in healing her core issue of inadequacy fostered in childhood by her mother.

When you sail back down the lifestream to the present, you may say to yourself, "Wait a minute. Why have I ended up at exactly the same point where I started? Nothing is different." Although your *outer* physical surroundings may look the same, you have shifted your *inner* emotional landscape because you have regained some piece of your energy.

Remember, regarding childhood changework, I talked about changing the inner reality, not the outer one. Lifestream works the same way. If you are dealing with a shame issue, your level of shame will have decreased because you removed a trigger that kept that piece of shame activated, and regained the life energy that was locked away.

This is what is so critical about this process. Regardless of what you believe, you have created a different reality, even though you do not suddenly find yourself in a different time and space. Sooner or later, when you return to the present after a lifestream journey, you *will* notice a difference around you, and most importantly in you.

You may not notice the difference today, next week, or next month, but sometime later you will realize that something that caused you shame no longer bothers you. What happened is that the feeling faded away slowly. Imagine that once the water remaining in the cut-off branch flowed away, no more replenished it.

As you continue working backward, cutting off the streams, you regain your lifeforce energy and build up enough strength to go further back and tackle the earlier splits. Eventually, you will have restored enough of your lifeforce to reach your oldest memories.

Your lifestream is your vitality, strength, feeling, power, self-ness; by regaining all of that, you are literally creating a new person. You no longer can remain your "old self" with old feelings and responses, since there is no longer any internal support or energy for that old self to exist.

Going Forward

Rivers often reach a floodplain. The water spreads out in rivulets and streamlets for quite a while, like a net. Eventually, the force of the water pouring in from behind pushes the river past the floodplain, and the streamlets merge again into one river.

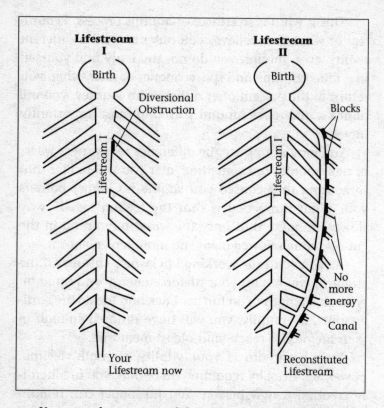

Lifestream I

Birth

Diversional Obstruction

Lifestream I

Your Lifestream now

Lifestream II

Birth

Blocks

Lifestream I

No more energy

Canal

Reconstituted Lifestream

You can change your lifestream by healing the river from your present position. Instead of going back up the stream to block off the original split, you can create a canal from your lifestream branch to others, so the life energy flows down into your river (see diagram, above). Using this technique does not require you to go back and release memories. It just declares, "I've had enough of that behavior; I'm going to reclaim myself now."

What you do is fold the rivulets back into the main river, using canals to create one river again. It does not matter which technique you choose to use—as long as things shift. You can work in both directions, since they both create powerful change.

The lifestream procedures can be done very easily. The effects, not as dramatic or as immediate as childhood or past life changework, are equally as profound in the long run.

EXERCISES

Going Back

1. Do your aura cleanout and bring yourself into present time.

2. Call in your Higher Self to assist you on this journey.

3. Summon a cloud, a helicopter, an enormous bird, or any other conveyance to move you upstream. Climb onto or into whatever shows up (the bird and cloud will be strong enough to hold you).

4. Instruct your Higher Self to guide your cloud/bird/ helicopter/boat, etc. back to the particular branch you wish to work on. (If you don't know, your Higher Self does.)

5. Proceed back up the lifestream until you see the split. It may get brighter; or you may feel a buzz or see a sign that says, "Here it is."

6. Look for the symbol that caused the split—a rock, ball, statue, sign, etc. Get rid of the object, with help from your Higher Self. Here are some examples:

    a. Have the angels toss it into the sun.

    b. Call in a huge golden ball to cover and dissolve the object.

    c. Let the earth open up a fissure and suck the object down into it.

7. Call in helpers (beavers, bulldozers, workers, etc.) to create a strong high dam across the branch that cannot be breached.

8. Watch the water in the branch flow away, never to be replenished, as the lifestream energy flows down to you.

9. Fly back downstream, and get off at your present time.

Going Forward

1. Do your aura cleanout and bring yourself into present time.

2. Call in your Higher Self to assist you on this journey.

3. Call in bulldozers, angels, whatever assistants you want, to create a canal between your river and another stream so the water from the branch flows into your river.

4. Watch the water flow into your river.

5. Put your feet in the river, and feel the new energy that has come back to you.

6. Repeat the exercise as often as you want.

CHAPTER 12

SEEING PAST LIVES

You have been working on issues from your present life. Now it's time to step back further into the past—the far past—into other lifetimes. I know you are probably aware of reincarnation and the idea that you have lived a series of consecutive lifetimes. Each of these lifetimes, even though you cannot remember them, has an impact on the choices you have made and experiences you have undergone, whether you are aware of them or not. In fact, once you start delving into the realm of past lives, much that may seem confusing or incomprehensible about your life suddenly becomes much clearer, such as the reason for a particular illness or deformity or experience.

Changing past lives can do just as much good as resolving your present life issues because your past lives contain traumas in the form of karmic debts, uncompleted agreements, or unfulfilled tasks that your soul would be more than grateful to discard.

If you could remember your past lives, you would recognize similarities between your present problems and the ones you had then, because all of your past lives have a direct correlation to present life issues. By recreating those experiences now, you're attempting to resolve them so they won't haunt you in the next life. Healing your childhood issues helps a great deal; but more can be done by past life work—which heals both that life and this one as well (two good deeds for the price of one). When you create a more positive outcome for your past lives, you no longer need to relive those mistakes over and over, lifetime after lifetime. Their effects in your present life will diminish—just like the dandelion dies after its taproot is removed.

How can you tell when you are dealing with a past life issue? Very simple. No matter how much you work on your problem, it never quite seems to get resolved. While present life changework nibbles at its edges, you can never get to its heart—until you go into a past life.

Except for the fact that they take place in different times and milieus, and with different costumes, past life dramas are timeless with the same emotional entanglements. Good or bad things happen to you, your family, and others around you; and after a life filled with a variety of experiences, you die in some way or other. That, of course, is the key difference from this present life so far; there was a terminus—your death.

The following is a good example of a typical past life scenario.

Case Study: Celia always felt abandoned by her family, no matter how strongly they professed their love. One day I asked her to follow that feeling of abandonment back to its source. She found herself as a young child with her mother, trapped in a burning cottage. Although her mother desperately tried to get them out, she was overcome by the smoke. As Celia, tears streaming down her face, watched this scenario unfold, she realized that her mother had really been trying to save her from the flames, though unsuccessfully, leaving the terrified child to perish abandoned and alone.

In your past lives, you will find that your parents, close friends, and significant others are closely intertwined with you, although it's not necessary that you recognize your mother from that lifetime as your child or spouse/lover in this one. You all switch roles from lifetime to lifetime, like a repertory company, creating all kinds of emotional interconnections and entanglements.

It may take a number of lifetimes to unsnarl the emotional knots because there is so much "juice" (unfinished business) among all of you which cannot reasonably be expected to get resolved in one lifetime, and in fact may be increased in the current life. By handling the situation back then, though, the problem won't continue to generate more energy in this life or the next. The result not only changes your life, sometimes dramatically, but it also affects all the other people involved as well.

Multiple Lives

Suppose that, instead of happening one after another, those "past lives" all exist simultaneously, even though they "appear" to take place over thousands of years. This idea of "simultaneous" lives was first described in the book *The Education of Oversoul Seven** which the entity Seth channeled to Jane Roberts. In this theory, linear time is only a construct, not a reality (with which Einstein would agree). I find it very apt in explaining changework because you can see the impact of the changes more easily.

Imagine a spoked wheel with a hub in the center. The hub is where your Oversoul lives, overseeing all the lifetimes, past, present, and future, and the spokes are your lifetimes. When a particular life gets activated (for example, by meeting someone who was with you in another lifetime—a spoke in your wheel), it comes down into the hub to be worked on. Any changes made to that lifetime then flow down all the spokes and alter the other lives accordingly. That means if you atone for being a miser in a past life, your relationship with money in other lives shifts. Or if you dissolve a sticky love agreement, that frees you both in all those lives where you two were lovers.

This ripple effect spreads throughout all of your collected life experience (including future lives on this planet, lives on other planets, and parallel lives). Although you only see its effects from the perspective of

---

* Jane Roberts. *The Education of Oversoul Seven* (Prentice-Hall, 1984).

here and now, if you had the opportunity to rise into your Oversoul, you could see the results radiate across the vast tapestry of your many lifetimes.

John Donne said, "No man [or woman] is an island." Although he was talking about human relationships, it applies to our many lifetimes as well. We do not exist in a vacuum; our motivations, needs, and fears connect to other lifetimes through our business associates, our family, our career, and our beliefs through lessons learned, gifts given, persons met, or a hundred other reasons.

Divine Help

When delving into your past lives, it is important to have at least one ally who is loving, caring, and strong, who sees you clearly and with complete love and acceptance, who can protect you from some of the personal "demons" who inhabit your past. That ally can be your Higher Self, a divine angel, or your Guardian Angel. Because they are in contact with all of your many lives, any of them can take you directly to the situation that resonates with this lifetime's issues.

Reactions

Just the idea of past life work may be provoking a strong inner reaction for some of you. First is your mind's loud objection to whatever you see or sense. When you find a past life, especially if you believe there's no such thing, that clear assault on your belief system can be shocking, particularly if the experience is very vivid and intense. Expect your mind to argue vociferously against the

141

validity of what you saw. That's all right as long as you don't succumb to its arguments and invalidate your experience. What's important is the *result*, whatever your belief.

Second, you may feel upset, angry, or embarrassed because what you see is unacceptable, unpleasant, or crazy. With its comments and judgments, your mind is getting in the way again. When one woman made a past life journey, she found herself on an asteroid trying to escape from aliens (she did believe in reincarnation, but not extraterrestrials). Once she got over her judgment about what she saw, she had a profound experience.

Finally, you may blame yourself for the terrible deeds your past life persona did, or get angry at how foolish your persona acted (of course you'd never do such a stupid thing), and want to have nothing to do with them ("They deserve to suffer!")—except that you're the one who's suffering now.

You may have any or all of those feelings before, during, and after the journey, and they still won't affect what goes on during the experience, as long as you are willing to process. You just need to work with whatever you see—and keep breathing. Your Higher Self manifested this scenario for your healing.

Karma

You can consider karma as a kind of cosmic balance sheet, listing your personal Accounts Payable (bad deeds) and Accounts Receivable (good deeds). No cosmic collection agency comes after you to hound you for those back debts, nor does God force you to pay up by causing you to burn in hell. It's your responsibility alone. Your Higher Self handles the repayment by finding some way for you to balance your debt.

After you die, your Higher Self assesses your life, dispassionately but lovingly, and tallies those karmic debts. If your good deeds outweighed the bad, you may be able to cancel some of your karma. For the debts that were not resolved or canceled, the soul then decides what kinds of lessons will give you an opportunity to complete the payback in another lifetime.

Very simply, that means if you hurt someone in one life, he or she gets to reciprocate in another. It may take many lifetimes for you to get up the nerve or strength to pay a particular debt (knowing that it will cause you pain), for you will have to put yourself into a situation where what you did to others gets done to you (sounds like the Golden Rule, doesn't it?). That's why people who rape and torture get abused and crippled by their erstwhile victims in another life.

Case Study: Dana had a very troubled relationship with her husband. Although she loved and supported him emotionally and financially, he had affairs and abused her emotionally all the time. When she looked for the past life that had necessitated this karmic payback, she discovered she had been a man, a wastrel and opportunist who seduced and married a rich, homely woman, then beat and mistreated her, whored around, squandered her fortune, and ultimately drove her to suicide. Her present life husband, who had been that woman, was exacting her retribution by doing the same thing to Dana now.

It's easier to watch lifetimes when you were the victim, not the villain. Unfortunately, each of us has a number of bad lifetimes, and usually one or two evil ones. (Bad means something like raping and pillaging, which has always been a generally acceptable, if unpleasant, reality in most societies throughout history; evil is Hitler and the Nazis, who actively pursued torture and genocide—there is a vast karmic difference.) In past life work, you get to see yourself exhibit all kinds of unpleasant behaviors.

> **Case Study:** For Ilene, no matter how much she worked on her childhood issues, she couldn't get past the belief that she "owed" her parents the right to hurt and abuse her. Although she could easily have absorbed such an idea during her childhood, that kind of statement smacked of karmic debt. When we followed her feeling back to its source, she saw a time when her parents were her slaves, whom she treated badly.

Having your rotten lives exposed can bring up shame over your less-than-stellar performance. Since you have severe judgments over your present day "faults," however large or small they might be, you may feel the impact even more when you find out about your bad deeds in your previous lives—which sometimes can be quite serious.

Immersed in your guilt, you need to remember that *you're watching an entirely different lifetime!* You are NOT that jerk, creep, lowlife, scum. If you are reading this book, you are a decent person trying to understand, heal, and evolve. You cannot afford to wallow in guilt and anguish over those past mistakes, but it will help if you accept your karma, pay it off, and move on.

What signals a "karmic debt"?

- The same issues come up over and over again with no measurable release.

- You keep talking about owing or guilt or obligation, or you have an almost obsessive need for payback, even if it isn't overtly expressed (severe codependency and addiction may be part of this issue. Addicts don't want to face the responsibility and concomitant pain of their karmic obligation).

- You have lots of intensity around the issue, far outweighing its importance.

When you've cleared the karmic debt, you will notice the following changes:

- A significant drop in your intensity around the issue.

- A significant drop in your obsessive need to owe or pay back, and a willingness to break free of old codependent or addictive patterns.

- An almost inexplicable but tangible feeling of relief, spreading throughout your body and soul.

Agreements

Agreements are dyad links forged between you and another person, usually for some purpose, and often for a particular time period. They include teacher/student, business associates, helpers, lovers—in other words, all the normal interpersonal connections you create in your life. They help you form bonds of support and caring that give your life meaning. Agreements may be short-lived (days, weeks, months), or extend for years or decades.

The problem arises when the agreements you made unwittingly remain in force across lifetimes. They have words like "always" and "never" and "forever" attached to them (as in "I'll love you forever," "We'll never let each other go"). "Forever" doesn't mean until you die, but for ever—lifetime after lifetime after lifetime.

Such unreleased bonds impede your growth and development by tying you two together, regardless of your present circumstances and development. That means what was once a viable relationship can turn into an imposition or burden, haunting you as an obsession or codependency, until you break the bond (or go nuts trying).

Many a person has found, when trying to shed a destructive relationship, that a "forever" chain holds the two parties together, trapping both of their energies in that age-old commitment. No matter how much work you do on yourself, nothing can really shift until your agreement is dissolved.

Case Study: Alicia was incapable of breaking up with a neglectful lover. She suffered endless heartache while he played around, yet could not give him up, even after extensive therapy to work on her dependency issues. In a past life, she heard herself swear to love this man forever, just before he went off to war and never came back. So here she was, holding on to that bond, lifetimes beyond its usefulness, and he was desperate to be free of her and it. Once she dissolved that agreement, it was amazingly easy for her to let her lover go and get on with her life—much to the relief of everyone involved.

Breaking an agreement is easy. You don't need a past life journey, just an understanding by the two participants to set each other free. (Some people become afraid that without an agreement, there will be nothing to hold the relationship together.) If either person feels any reluctance or fear that the relationship (such as it is) will vanish without that hook, just remember that you cannot create a healthy connection with a messy agreement in the way. If you two do break up subsequent to dissolving the agreement, it was overdue for termination—and any reason for staying together is long gone. It's time to move on.

• • •

CHAPTER 13

CHANGING A PAST LIFE

Right now you may want only to find out what happened during one of your lifetimes; after all, it takes time to adjust to the idea of past lives (although I've found that a lot of people who are wary of the concept are intensely curious about their own past lives). It's perfectly fine for you to simply make that choice—at least at the beginning. On the other hand, you may find that an earlier lifetime has a serious impact on your present life. If you are willing to change the story as you did with your childhood memories, you can apply your modern perceptions, your Higher Self's innate wisdom, and/or angelic love, toward creating a new, positive result in that life—and in this one.

The first step is to locate a past life—and the most effective way to do that is identical to discovering a present life trauma: by following the body sensation back to its first occurrence in your soul's experience, whenever that is. It's like reeling in a taut fishing line and hauling up the fish that's hooked on the end. The more intense the feeling, the more easily you can follow it back to its source. Celia, who wanted to go to the origin of her abandonment issue, ended up dying in a burning cottage (which was completely beyond her expectation).

Even though your mind may convince you otherwise, you can reach a past life. It takes willingness. If you worry about finding a past life during your first attempts, I suggest a mild self-hypnotic induction that you can imagine for yourself—as you hold your Higher Self's hand, slowly go down a staircase and open a door into your past. The door signals a clear demarcation of realities, moving from an outer, logical world into the inner, magical, non-logical universe where all things are possible.

Ask your Higher Self to take you to the major crisis/decision point of your life. Once you and your Higher Self step through the doorway, take a few moments to get a sense of the situation. It's like watching a play or a movie. What's happening? Who are the major characters or personae? What is the situation or problem? Who is doing what to whom? You may get an image or simply a feeling.

One woman said, "I don't see a thing, but I'm terrified of being here. Someone is trying to kill me." (Her Higher Self moved her to safety immediately.) Ask for help if you feel you need it. That's why your Higher Self accompanies you on these journeys, to remind you that you are never alone and resourceless or helpless.

Do not imagine what you *ought* to see. Just allow whatever comes up to be there. Your mind will try, as usual, to get in the way with its comments, especially if you have some knowledge of a particular time period. Just thank it and continue. *Do not make assumptions or create an expected scenario.* Let it unravel on its own. I'm continually surprised by what people come up with, and the stories are rarely what they (or I) expect. Trust that your Higher Self knows that what it's showing you is right.

You may find yourself merging with your past life persona, as you merged with your Inner Child, so that you are actually in the scene. Usually, I don't encourage that. It's important to remain a separate, invisible observer. There are two reasons for this. 1) If the event is traumatic, just as from your childhood, you can get overwhelmed by the drama; and 2) if you stay merged with your persona, you begin to see with that persona's world view. Changing a past life situation requires your modern perspective, so remain separate.

If you find yourself merged with your persona, imagine stepping out of that body and standing across from it, or have your Higher Self take your hand and separate you from your persona.

Watch the story unfold as if it were on videotape, so you can observe what happens with some neutrality: "I see my character being killed by brigands." "I'm raping and pillaging that poor defenseless village." That may mean watching your own death. You will have a chance to rewrite your life once you have seen what happened. It's like rewinding the videotape, then editing in your changes.

Making Changes

There are two kinds of past life changes you would normally make: 1) saving someone (usually yourself) from harm, or 2) resolving/healing karmic issues. Either one involves intervention of some sort in the lifetime.

Case Study: Celia (of the burning cottage) wanted to save her mother and herself—the child. Her Higher Self said, "Turn around and look for the door." The next thing I heard was, "We're safe!" When she came back from her journey, Celia said, "I'm amazed at what happened. As soon as I saw that door, my mother grabbed me and tore out of there." She added, "I understand now that my mother loved me. She didn't abandon me intentionally."

My rule of thumb for all my work (in past and present lifetimes) is "go for safety." Make your persona safe before doing anything else. Surprisingly, just doing that can cause an enormous shift (since that often means saving them from death).

Case Study: Ellen consistently got trapped in dangerous situations (both emotional and physical) in this lifetime. In searching for a reason, she found a past life, where she saw her persona stoned to death by the neighbors in her village who feared her because she was "different" (not part of their village). Ellen decided that her persona had to leave that place to be safe, i.e., survive. To reconfigure that lifetime, Ellen guided her persona to the river where a boat was waiting to take her persona to another, safer village. Then she watched the persona marry, raise a family, and die, after a totally different life from the trapped, traumatic lifetime she actually "lived."

Suggestions

If you want to change that scenario, you need to do it wisely, so that the results will be satisfactory for that time—and for you here and now. Some kinds of change are simple, as in Celia's case—finding a way out of the burning cottage and having her mother take her away. That was what she needed to break the hold of her abandonment issue. She still had present life feelings to resolve, but the root cause had been removed. Other solutions are more complex.

If you showed your modern self to a person living in the Middle Ages and said, "Hi, you need to follow my instructions," he'd be convinced you were the devil leading him into hell. That's because his world view allows for only two kinds of supernatural beings—angels and devils, and since all strangers are devils, you must be one. To get around that, you must present yourself as some kind of authority figure in the metaphor of the time.

One of the key factors in successful past life work is the ability to blend into the situation in order to take control of the action. For example, presenting yourself to that medieval persona as an angel would be eminently acceptable; to someone in ancient times, you could be a goddess, god, or nature spirit.

In the inner world, you can make all kinds of suggestions to further or change the action, for they are accepted as *totally normal*, as long as they are consistent with the scenario. When I've made a suggestion like, "Go find the door and leave now," I've rarely had a client say, "There's no such thing." Rather they see it, open it, and walk right through, like Celia did.

If your mind questions the legitimacy of those suggestions, I say something like, "In the inner world everything is possible." That sentence does a lot to calm your mind, which needs to make logical sense of what is going on (as best it can under the circumstances).

When you tie your suggestions to the internal logic of the period, you will have no problem incorporating them into the story. Anachronisms definitely cause concern. In other words, no airplanes, telephones, or jet fighters in prehistoric times.

> **Case Study:** In a lifetime in Atlantis, Maris heard and saw a telephone ringing. After some discussion with me about it, she decided that since Atlantis was a technologically advanced civilization, maybe they did have telephones. Only after coming to that conclusion could she continue with her process. [I suspect Atlantis is an exception.]

You will not go wrong at any time by asking your Higher Self or an angel for suggestions, such as, "What do I do next?" Your Higher Self will give you very detailed and clear answers like, "Find the door." Pass those instructions on to your persona. It's rare that your persona will argue with you. If he or she does, remind them that whatever they've done so far hasn't worked very well. If necessary, take the persona's hand and

guide him or her to wherever you want them to go, as
Ellen did.

> **Case Study:** Martha always wanted to be top dog
> in every kind of relationship with men. In going
> to the source of her fierce need for control, she saw
> herself as a priestess for the goddess religion at the
> time when the warriors of the patriarchal religion
> conquered her village, which included the chief
> raping her. Unable to fight him off physically, she
> shut him off emotionally. She vowed she would
> never again be put in such a powerless position
> (i.e., *forever*).
>
> After viewing the situation, she and her Higher
> Self formulated a different outcome. Since both
> the priestess and warrior recognized that change
> was inevitable, and neither liked the obvious solu-
> tion, Martha, in goddess form, suggested an alter-
> native—that the priestess and the warrior treat
> each other with respect instead of brutality and
> contempt, and turn the "rape" into a "joining of
> forces." Not only did both parties gratefully accept
> this solution (the priestess was attracted to the
> chieftain), Martha experienced a marked shift in
> her own attitude toward men.

After you've made your changes with your persona,
sit back and watch the persona's new life unfold as if it
were a TV movie. This last step is particularly critical, and
eminently satisfying, as you see how their life improved
after you rescued them from disaster. You don't have to
do any work. (It's like watching a ball roll down a hill;
once it has its initial push, it rolls all by itself.)

Karmic Payback

If you see a life in which you were the victim, you'll gladly create a new outcome that saves your persona from some dire fate. However, if your persona is the perpetrator of much anguish, you're going to feel other kinds of emotion (like shame, guilt, and anger) for what you did, as you watch him or her in action. Making the necessary changes is going to be hard because you're going to have a difficult time remaining neutral or non-judgmental.

> **Case Study:** Louise was a spiritual junkie; she took every metaphysical workshop and class around, desperately trying to unlock her psychic powers. While all her friends were having psychic visions, doing channeling, seeing auras—all the things she could only dream about, nothing seemed to work for her. In looking for the cause of her inability to open psychically, she learned that she was under a karmic "curse." In other lifetimes, she had used her powerful psychic powers for evil purposes. Her punishment now was to have them locked away when she really wanted to use them for good. This punishment caused her enormous anguish; yet she recognized it was a fitting karmic atonement.

Watching a lifetime like that will be painful, but you can get some respite by stopping the process and returning to it later on when you feel strong enough to continue. There's no deadline or timetable for doing changework. Just tell your Higher Self that you want to stop working on the past life for now. It will put the process into limbo until you're ready. Even if you do continue working on it, no matter how painful, just keep breathing deeply. It helps release your energy.

Luckily, you don't have to do this changework alone. Let angels or your Higher Self handle any punishment and rectification while you watch. They will be decent, caring, and dispassionate. If you want to participate, treat the incident like you were dealing with childhood abuse. Asking the question, "What needs to be done to this abuser so that he atones for his deeds?" Your Higher Self will provide the appropriate answer, as usual.

Your persona must be punished. It's important that he pay off as much karmic debt as possible, then and there, by suffering in some way. Sometimes the persona will go further and acknowledge his or her wickedness and accept atonement for their bad deeds; and sometimes they will refuse. When that happens, it means you're stuck with the payback by "suffering" the consequences in your present life. Yet that doesn't have to be a final answer; you can always check in later and see if you've paid enough.

Karmic work creates the most intense resolution because it exposes you to your worst and most unpleasant selves. Conversely, the payoff for completing it is the highest. Releasing karma not only frees up *enormous* energy, but it shatters many internal patterns for good. Every piece you resolve creates great big chunks of healing in your soul, as well as in your life.

Angels can also forgive karmic debt if they deem it appropriate. You can ask them from time to time whether they will forgive any of your outstanding karmic debt or determine when you have paid enough.

When you have completed your karma, it's very easy to recognize and experience it. It feels like a vast wave of relief, gratitude, and sadness sweeping through you, taking away pain—and leaving you light and joyous (until the next issue arises).

Is It Real?

After any past life experience is over, you may have several questions: Was it real? Did it really happen that way? And did it make a difference? Your logical mind may argue that changing the past life doesn't make rational sense (if it wasn't just your imagination). *It doesn't matter.* What is important is not the *label* you place on the experience, but the *experience* itself. You can't go back to that lifetime except in your mind (those folks are long dead!).

In any case, that's not the important criterion. Did you experience some kind of change or transformation? Did you emerge with a different understanding or feeling? Those are the criteria for measuring meaningful change. By providing whatever support your persona needs to choose a different option for his or her life, the experience ceased to be incomplete and was healed inside *you*, where it all matters. In almost every case where clients healed a past life, they underwent some kind of tangible shift in this life as well.

By healing a past life trauma, you free up centuries of trapped energy for your use now. You get to see and feel a result in that life, and inside you now.

Moreover, the benefits of past life work go far beyond just you. When you untangle a past life knot, other people involved get healed too, whether they know it or not. You are truly part of a large interconnecting network of relationships. When you shift, so does everyone else. Although the results may not be obvious, at least at first, they will become apparent as the months go by. Since you have healed the emotional entanglement, you can proceed to create other, healthier connections with those persons if you choose, or disconnect from them permanently this time, without hostility, anger, or karma.

EXERCISES

Healing a Past Life

1. Call in your Higher Self or Guardian Angel. Instruct them to take you to the appropriate lifetime.

2. See a flight of stairs leading to a door.

3. Hand in hand with them, go down the stairs. Say, "I am going back to the first occurrence of (fill in your issue)." With each step you move back years or centuries to the first occurrence of your issue.

4. At the bottom is the door that takes you directly to the lifetime you are looking for. Step through into that lifetime.

5. Be the unseen observer in the scene. If you have merged with the persona, separate yourself. You need to see this story with modern eyes. Ask your

Higher Self to take your hand and pull you out of the persona's body if you need to.

6. Watch the story unfold. If you aren't seeing or feeling anything, ask that your Higher Self bring you to the critical event.

7. Watch what happens. That may mean seeing your persona's death.

Just doing these steps may be enough for you at this time. If you wish to continue and release the trauma, follow the next few steps.

1. Rewind the past life "videotape" to a time before the event (like your death).

2. Find a way to get your persona out of the painful or deadly situation.

3. If you have no suggestions, ask your Higher Self. It knows what to do next. Follow its advice. That may mean becoming visible in a way that fits the society to give advice to the persona ("find the door," "follow the path").

4. If your persona is the villain, ask your Higher Self to handle any punishment so that you don't have to get involved in the process.

5. Show or give the persona appropriate props, like a boat or a door, a tool to further guide him to a safe haven.

6. Observe the newly reconstructed life until the persona's death. That is very important because it gives that life and your soul a sense of completion.

7. Thank your Higher Self, and come back up the stairs.

If you are concerned about the process, have a friend read these instructions to you or put them on tape (or you can order a tape from me that outlines this whole process).

Breaking Your Agreement

1. Close your eyes and imagine yourself in a sacred outdoor space. Be sure there is a campfire burning.

2. Ask that your Higher Self join you and bring the agreement you want to break. Visualize it as a piece of paper with writing.

3. Invite the other party to join you at the campfire with her or his Higher Self and bring the written agreement.

4. Ask the other party if she or he is willing to dissolve the connection. If they show any reluctance, remind them of the mess the agreement has made of both your lives.

5. Write "Canceled" on your agreement. Tear it up, and burn the pieces in the fire.

6. Say, "I release you" three times.

7. Watch as the other party does the same. You have disconnected yourselves from each other.

8. Say goodbye.

You may do this exercise without involving the other person. Just omit steps 3, 4, and 6. Some people like to do it unilaterally, while others find it useful to face their agreement partner on the inner plane to say goodbye. It's your preference. Either way, the agreement gets broken.

•••

CHAPTER 14

CORE ISSUES: THE SOUL

After all your work on yourself, are you experiencing a certain level of frustration at your seeming lack of progress? Do you keep stumbling over a basic issue that appears intractable—no matter how diligently you work on it? No matter what you do, it recurs again and again and again, often at deeper levels of intensity. Congratulations! You have reached the core issue of your life. It permeates your entire being, and affects everything you do and think.

Your core issue, a basic belief about yourself and the world, is the primary motivator of your life. It is so overwhelming, powerful, and inherent in you at a cellular level, that your whole life is controlled and colored by it. It transcends mere abuse and dysfunction, which only reinforce its control over you.

I have briefly mentioned core beliefs in earlier chapters, but now it's time to discuss them in much more detail and put them into a larger perspective. There are three basic core issues or fears: fear of death, fear of abandonment, and fear of loss of self-identity, which derive from an unfulfilled need—for safety, for love, or for being yourself—something essential that is missing from your life and your soul.

A person with the fear of death defines life according to survival: "Will I be safe or will I be destroyed?" A person who fears abandonment defines life according to love: "Will I get love, or be left with none?" A person who fears loss of self defines life according to personal space: "Will I have the right to be myself, or will someone intrude and take away my identity?" These core beliefs may not seem obvious in your daily life, but they underlie your behavior, your feelings, your beliefs, and every one of your decisions and actions. Moreover, because of that unfulfilled need, it's not hard to believe that you are worthy of anything that would provide you with safety, love, or self-identity. Everything you think, do, or believe is in reaction to your core belief, either striving to counter its influence, or succumbing to that belief.

The decision you make about the world, based on your environment in the first twelve months of your life, forms the foundation of your belief system. You then spend the next two years solidifying this belief. That means if you spent your early months of life with an abusive family, but you were removed from that home and put into a loving, caring household, you probably had a very good chance of not absorbing a core fear about survival. If, however, the harmful situation persisted well into the first three years, it was very difficult for you to break that belief because the fear of death had become cemented into your cells.

The Three Core Beliefs

Death

When you have a core issue around survival, you judge everything according to your safety. If you live in a war zone (whether it's in the inner city, a war-torn country, or a violent or rage-filled household), you are in terror for your life. That fear of death creates a belief that you don't deserve to be alive, and, because of that, you don't deserve to have anything. People with this belief are often filled with rage (that they either express or suppress) in order to stay alive. For you, survival is crucial.

All of your decisions, no matter how small, are life and death decisions. You deal with black and white, rather than with shades of gray. Children see the world in absolutes, and so do adults with the fear of death. Normally, as you grow up, you learn to compromise and negotiate to get your needs met. You can function well—until you run into a threatening situation which throws you into survival mode. Then you react from your core fear. At a time like that, you don't worry about how much better it might be if you negotiated the issue. For you, it's all or nothing. Life or death. Those are the only alternatives.

There's a saying, "Half a loaf is better than none." Not if you're in survival mode. You can't have half a loaf because half a loaf means death. There is no half-life or half-death. It's all or nothing.

Abandonment

If, as a baby, you got only your bodily needs met, you will always be hungering for what you are missing—enough love and attention to fill that hole left by neglect and abandonment. When you feel abandoned, you believe you are unworthy of having anything, particularly love. This is a description of abandonment.

For you, the loaf symbolizes love, which you *know* is unattainable. While the survivor clutches onto the loaf for dear life, you have no loaf at all, except for a few crumbs. In fact, you'd gladly give away even those crumbs if it meant that someone would let you shower them with attention (in the hope that they'd give you back some small modicum of love).

That's why people who have an abandonment issue are often codependents and caregivers; they'll endure all kinds of abuse in hope of gaining approval (i.e., love) whether or not the other person had it to give in the first place. Unfortunately, abandoned people usually attract partners who are indifferent to their needs for affection and want instead to be alone because of their core issue, which is loss of self.

Loss of Self

If you sense people grabbing at you, demanding that you pay attention to them, or intruding on your space, you believe you have no place that you can call your own—even your own self. You always have the fear that you are going to be jumped or intruded on by someone. Your body, your mind, even your soul are under siege. (You need to do the exercises in Chapter 5.) Hence, you are afraid that you have no right to be your own person. (The abandoned ones reading this book will have a hard time understanding this core issue, which is diametrically opposite to their need. What they wouldn't give for such a situation!)

As a baby you might have been fussed over constantly, or raised among a lot of other people in the household so that your boundaries were constantly invaded. You were rarely allowed any privacy or time for yourself, nor did you feel that you were allowed by your caregivers to create your own identity.

To you, the loaf symbolizes your self that you want to clutch protectively against your chest. "I won't give it to you," you declare. Because of that, you may often be labeled as selfish, but you're afraid of giving away part of your self. Sharing it without your agreement or permission equals invasion, so you set up strong, sometimes harsh boundaries to protect yourself.

Even with such high barriers, you still continue to worry that you're not strong enough to fend off outsiders and their assault on your identity. You are afraid a part of you will be removed. That's why you are very quick to defend your territory with "Do Not Trespass" signs. "Leave me alone! I don't trust you!" These phrases often recur in your speech when you have activated this core belief. It's going to take a lot of trust-building before you can even create a doorway through your walls, never mind tearing them down. That takes a long time.

Lack of Love and Trust

These three basic core issues revolve around the lack of love and trust. You live in fear of its happening again and again (being destroyed, left, or smothered). If you aren't protected, you alternate between rage and acquiescence; if you feel abandoned, you reach out to grab anyone available for love; if you feel smothered and invaded, you need to create barriers for protection. In none of these cases can you trust that you will get your needs met by someone else, so you're always hypervigilant, on the lookout for those situations or people that will trigger your core-issue fear.

> **Case Study:** Jane was a codependent, always taking care of Marvin, who felt like he was being smothered by her. She was always underfoot, mooning over him, and begging for love. When she did that, Marvin retreated. Jane was the abandoned child begging for love, while Marvin needed his space. The result was that the more he withdrew from her, the more frantically Jane threw herself at him. The situation worsened to the point that Marvin never wanted to come home, which drove Jane into desperation and terror that he would leave.

This example describes a very common couple dynamic—of the giver and the taker—who exhibit the core issues of abandonment and loss of self. Healing this relationship meant finding ways for them to address and satisfy the other's core issue, such as creating time for them to do things together so Jane would feel loved, and time for Marvin alone, so he wouldn't feel smothered, and the creation of other activities for Jane that would allow her to stop fixating on Marvin and his needs. After a while, Marvin began to miss Jane's company and began paying more loving attention to her without her urging.

> **Case Study:** For Greg, marriage had an all-or-nothing quality. If there was any kind of argument, he just knew that Elaine would leave; so no matter what he really believed, he acquiesced to her ideas, and swallowed his anger. Finally, one day, he blew up during a minor disagreement; she was absolutely stunned by his shocking behavior, which seemed to come out of nowhere.
>
> When Greg said that he thought if he got angry, she'd leave, Elaine was shocked. Her response was, "I always thought you never cared enough about me to bother to give me your opinion—or show an emotion." He countered, "But if you didn't like what I would say, you'd get mad and leave." He saw everything, large or small, in terms of an all-or-nothing, black-and-white situation.

To Greg, conflict plugged into his life/death issue, so he couldn't see any alternative except Elaine's leaving if they had an argument.

(See how easy it is to interpret other people's motives according to our core issues!) To help Greg feel safer, they set up rules for communication. They also learned each other's expectations about conflict. He began to realize that an argument didn't mean the end of the relationship (death); it just meant that there was a disagreement. They could still remain together.

The True Depth of Core Issues

When you trigger your core issue, your only motivation is to create safety for yourself in whatever way you have chosen. For example, when you are threatened by what you perceive as a life-threatening situation, you will automatically drop into a flight/fight mode. Or if you are feeling abandoned, you will be in terror over the loss of love; or if you are feeling smothered, you will pull yourself behind a high wall. Nothing can snap you out of that fear until you remove yourself from the situation—or the cause of the fear disappears.

Under most conditions, the nurturing love and joy that radiates from your Higher Self or angels can penetrate into you, like the warmth from a cheery fire. However, when you are gripped by a core issue, it is almost impossible to feel anything until you remove the stimulus.

If you believe that you are going to be destroyed, abandoned, or smothered, all the nurturing you get from your Higher Self and angels cannot penetrate through your haze of terror. Processing, inner support systems, and self-comforting will be unsuccessful until your adrenaline stops pumping, and you come back into reality and see that the world is not as fearful as you've been feeling. Only then can you feel clear enough to accept comfort from your Higher Self and the angels.

Why is your core issue so potent and so intractable to normal processing? When you discover your particular core belief, you may sense a familiarity about it; that's because you have lived with it for a long time. It does not exist simply in this lifetime. It has dominated most of your lives—and will continue to do so in future lifetimes until you resolve it. That's why simply working on it in present time doesn't break you free of its bonds. It emanates from your very soul.

Present life processing is like cleaning out one abscess after another, without addressing the whole system (like western medicine, which deals only with the symptom, not the whole person). In the same way, present life therapy addresses the symptom (childhood). Only past life work really confronts the whole problem, letting you reach a point where you are cleaning out core issues at the very basic level of your being, at soul level.

If you were to ask your Higher Self to take you back to the earliest occurrence of a core issue, you would find yourself in a past life, and not just any past life—an early, early life. Core issue lifetimes are usually short—no more than three to five years long. Often, you barely made it out of the womb. Just like the major issues of this life took time to settle in, so it was in the past. It took several lifetimes, one after another, to cement the core issue into your soul. These fears were then reinforced in later lifetimes until they became an integral part of your soul.

Case Study: Every one of Dierdre's relationships had brought up her issues of abandonment. Her lovers demanded that she please them, and if she didn't, they'd leave. Finally, fed up with this abuse, and after much counseling on her abandonment issue, she decided to find the root of her crippling abandonment issue. During past life work, she went to one of the first lives after she decided to become a human being—very, very long ago.

She saw a deformed newborn baby being abandoned by its mother, who projected tremendous disgust and repulsion at the baby's deformity. These emotions appeared as a viscid green slime that covered its body. Not only was the infant left to die, but the abandonment was overlaid with repulsion and disgust that made Dierdre feel utterly worthless and unloved.

Dierdre's first task was to clean off the green slime from the baby. Then, with help from her Higher Self, she gave the baby to a couple who were delighted with the child, regardless of its deformity.

Case Study: Lisa saw herself as a baby looking up at the blue sky. Suddenly a face with large sharp fangs came down over her head and ate her up. At that moment she felt shock and terror at her death. Her soul saw her mother, who had put the baby down on the grass, wail in horror and grief at losing her child to the predator cat. Lisa, of course, considers the world a dangerous place.

Such core issue life stories are not unusual.

Warning Signs

When you are caught up by a core issue, you may not realize what's going on with you. Here are some warning signs to tip you (and your friends) off.

- You obsess about something (or someone) constantly, day and night. You simply cannot let it go. It creates enormous emotional turmoil inside you.

- You feel completely ungrounded, unconnected to your Higher Self, Source, the angels, or to the earth. Nor can you ground yourself into reality, no matter what you do.

- You can't see your core issue clearly, nor do you have the ability to find any clarity. It's as if you're on a carousel spinning out of control. You have no balance or neutrality.

- This terror is beyond your Inner Child. In fact, your Inner Child itself is being buffeted by huge waves of chaos that are overwhelming you, and its terror adds more intensity to your own fear. Having your Higher Self or an angel comfort the Child will take some of the pressure off you while you're lost in your terror.

If you can recognize the times you are activated, then you can take steps to remove the fear-producing stimulus (for example, leaving the dangerous situation, finding a supportive, loving friend, retreating to a safe, private place) so you can reach an inner feeling of safety. Only then can you regain your adult equilibrium.

The Consequences of Change
It's one thing to wrestle with the core issue in this lifetime; to go back and heal it in those early lifetimes means you are committed to changing something deeply profound inside of you—an essential piece of the being that you are, something that you have known, loved, and cherished for most of your existence on earth. Your core issue has become part of the makeup of

your soul. By chipping away at it, you are gradually changing into someone else—someone you don't know. That can be very intimidating. What kind of person are you likely to become?

When you work with the lifestream, you shouldn't go back upstream to the very first split until you've processed some of the branches closer to the present. That won't cause a radical shift in your energy, which would be dangerously disruptive to all your bodies (one consequence is that you will probably get pretty sick). It takes time and effort to prepare yourself for such a dramatic energy shift. Core issues are exactly the same. Tackle the later lives first. When you've re-created enough of them and resolved their issues, then you can handle the profound changes that will develop out of your core issue changework.

The earlier the lifetimes you work with, the stronger the payoff in this lifetime because you're going deeper and deeper into your soul. As you reconfigure those lives, you will find yourself having fewer inherent constraints on your beliefs, your attitudes, your behavior, and your feeling toward yourself.

Moving Backward

When you feel ready to tackle a core issue, you can use the past life technique described in Chapter 13. Ask your Higher Self to bring you to one of the first times in which you experienced survival-fear, abandonment, or loss of self. As usual, the easiest way to access these early past lives is to follow your body sensation. If you are experiencing core issue terror, you can use that to guide you back to the original experience (or one very soon after).

Observe the life with your Higher Self beside you. Just watch the lifetime, even if you don't feel strong enough to make any changes. Simply observing the events may be all you can endure at the start. (It's quite remarkable the intensity of emotion these lives evoke because they appear so simple and uncomplicated; but their impact on you is so profound.) You can re-create the lifetime at another time.

I cannot emphasize enough how critical core issue work is. It is profound, monumental, and daunting. Therefore, for some of your changework you may require the assistance of a good therapist to help you confront your deepest issues, most particularly a Transpersonal therapist who is receptive to working with past lives, present problems, the Higher Self and angels, and the Inner Child.

In addition, you can provide your own self-support. One of the keys is to begin affirming that you are acceptable and okay (with the reassurance of your Higher Self and angels). Another key is to create situations that support self-acceptability, including participating in activities with acquaintances you enjoy, developing your own ability to create safety in your environment, and recognizing that your gifts are worthy of being shared with others. All this will help you reshape your attitudes about yourself and your core issue. As you do it, it becomes much easier to let go of your old behaviors and beliefs.

What does a person who is free of their core issue look like? Happy. Relaxed. At peace. Loving. It's hard to know. Most of us aren't there. A clue to what it looks like is how you act when you are feeling comfortable, at ease, and in control and happy with yourself. The fear of death, abandonment, and self-loss sweeps over you less and less often. That means, in core issue situations, you may still revert to that terror, but the frequency and duration drop significantly as time goes on. Under most circumstances, you can act as an adult, not a terrified child. To me that is a measure of progress—that you can keep the control of yourself more and more in your adult hands. That's a major step in healing.

•••

CHAPTER 15

PHOBIAS: THE AURA

What is it you fear most? Is there a reason for your fear? Or is it inexplicable, seemingly irrational, at least to others?

Some of us harbor unreasonable fears of spiders or snakes, or cats, or sleep, or the number 13, or high or small places, or that we'll be squashed to death, or a hundred and one other terrors. There is no logical reason for these terrors, so they are labeled as phobias.

The dictionary describes a phobia as a persistent, irrational, abnormal or intense fear of something without any obvious cause (the word means "fear" in Greek). Some familiar phobias include agoraphobia (fear of open spaces and crowds), acrophobia (fear of heights), and claustrophobia (fear of small enclosed places), or fear of going over bridges or being in an airplane. Some phobias are suffered by only a few people, others are much more common (like claustrophobia). Some of us can cope with them in our everyday lives while others of us are incapacitated by our phobias.

When you are in the grip of a phobia, you cannot think clearly. Your brain is wired in such a way that the stimulus completely bypasses your logical mind and goes straight into the reptilian brain, triggering a wildly extreme physical body reaction. Your heart races and pounds and your legs turn to jelly; you are beyond emotion or reason. Terror courses through you. You only want to flee.

People who experience an earthquake or survive the unrelenting horror of war, or develop claustrophobia from a situational trigger such as being shut into a closet when they were small suffer from post-traumatic stress, a strong emotional reaction to that event that can be resolved over time with therapy. Phobias, on the other hand, with their intensely strong body reactions, don't seem to have an obvious trigger in this life experience. The fear has always been with you.

I am acrophobic, but nothing in my past explains why I suffer from it. How did I get it? No one in my family knows; I have never been in a situation where I was at a great height as a child (I didn't climb trees until I was older). I rarely find my phobia a problem simply because I tend to avoid heights. When I happen to look down from a high place, I get a rush of terror, my legs turn to gelatin, and I see myself falling off the cliff or building, and landing at the bottom in a bloody mush.

Sometimes when I feel brave, I attempt to confront my acrophobia. It once took me about a half hour to climb up 140 steps to an ancient kiva in Bandelier National Park. It was very hard to inject some rationality or calmness through my terror, but I just kept breathing deeply and meditating to calm myself, while a friend massaged my shoulders to help me relax. Eventually, I made it to the top, but I remember every single step I took.

The psychotherapeutic community has wrestled with phobias for a long time. Talk therapy is woefully unsuccessful, as Freud himself found out. The only recognized successful treatment is behavioral modification through gradual sensory desensitization (to the great irritation of classically trained psychotherapists). It works like this: If you are afraid of bridges, you first learn to relax (using deep breathing and meditation techniques). Then you are shown a picture of a bridge (the stimulus). As your normal terror reaction kicks in, you use your relaxation techniques to calm down. When the terror becomes too intolerable, you remove the picture and relax. Gradually, you increase your tolerance of the bridge picture. Then the stakes are upped. You drive by a bridge, and when you can handle that, you stop at the bridge, and so on.

Behavior modification works by desensitizing the symptom, not resolving the issue. Only symptom relief is done to lessen your reaction to the stimulus (which is the stated goal of behavior modification). You overcome the debilitating effects of the terror, so you can function without being overwhelmed.

The origin of the terror can never be addressed or removed because phobias have no triggering mechanism in this lifetime; they come from some past life experience. Standard past life work focuses on repairing incomplete issues or repaying karmic debts that relate to your present life situation. The repercussions of that unfinished business still resonate in your emotional body by re-creating similar circumstances in your other lifetimes until the issue gets resolved, but they do not provoke the soul-searing terror that a phobia creates.

Somehow, in a past lifetime, you had an experience that traumatized your soul. Usually it had to do with a violent form of death. Now your soul reacts in terror when the situation is re-created in some way (like a claustrophobic walking into an elevator). Because of having that violent experience of death, your life's work may not have been completed; moreover, you still suffer a death trauma that remains unresolved.

Case Study: Harvey had an irrational fear of enclosed areas (claustrophobia); and every time he stepped into an elevator or closet, he felt a rush of panic so strong that he was afraid he would start choking to death. This panic persisted, even after years of psychotherapy in a fruitless search for the cause. Only behavior modification relieved the symptomatic terror.

Eventually, wanting to get to the root of the phobia, he decided to do past life work. Almost immediately, he found himself trapped in a dark cave that had collapsed, crushing his chest so he could not breathe. He died of asphyxiation. As soon as Harvey saw that, he reshaped the memory by getting someone to rescue him so he survived the cave-in; as a result, his claustrophobia disappeared.

Etheric Energy

Parapsychologists and psychics who investigate haunted houses often find that the ghosts who inhabit such dwellings were killed violently, or suffered a fatal accident so abruptly and unexpectedly that they did not fully realize that they had died. They were in a kind of shock; while their essence (Higher Self/Soul) moved on, their etheric body (aura) remained stuck in that location on the physical earth plane, still believing that they were alive. When the psychics helped the ghosts recognize that their body was dead, the auras no longer had any connection to that place and could then dissipate; most did so.

Not only do you experience an extraordinary shock if your death is violent, you depart your dead body without bringing away all of your essence. Your etheric body gets stuck in that one place, so you lose that piece of energy from your soul. That means you are incomplete when you move on to the next lifetime.

If you don't reclaim your etheric energy in the next lifetime (and you probably won't because you don't know that something is missing), the trauma remains embedded, lifetime after lifetime, so that whenever a resonating or similar situation arises, the soul immediately reacts. This is what creates the phobia.

Not only was your soul traumatized by your auric loss, it was also traumatized by the violent experience that caused it. That's another mark of a phobia—an enormous rush of adrenaline that floods the body and soul, searing the soul at that moment with incredible fear.

181

When your soul takes possession of a new body, it immediately imprints that body with its terror and loss. Over many lifetimes the soul's loss gets stamped on each physical body as an intense irrational fear. There is no mental or emotional link, nor is the phobia something your mental and emotional bodies can understand or deal with. The phobia is mysterious and irrational.

Clearing Phobias

Clearing a phobia requires going back to heal the past life, using the intensity of the terror as the key or fishing line back to the past life, and resolving the original experience. When you do so, the piece of the soul that was lost can finally be retrieved by your soul. I have discussed mental, physical, and emotional healing in other chapters. Resolving a phobia is a soul/aura healing. You have reclaimed a piece of your aura that was missing, and in so doing, freed the soul from an incredible trauma. When you finally heal that experience, the imprinted trauma can leave the soul's structure.

When Harvey created a different outcome for his life story by having someone rescue his persona, not only did he resolve his death, but he healed the trauma in his soul by retrieving that missing piece of himself. After doing his changework, he was able to go into elevators without the constant terror of choking. His soul's anguish had healed, after many lifetimes.

That kind of changework causes powerful alterations in your brain patterns, just like changing childhood traumas affects your Inner Child. The neuron pathways leading to that event get disconnected so that your body doesn't react the same way. The phobia provokes the manufacture of adrenaline, the fight/flight hormone, which remains in the cells for some time after an episode frightens them.

Because the physical body bears the brunt of the trauma every time the phobia gets triggered, it still retains the imprint of that soul's trauma, but the underlying terror has been removed. The result is that you may feel some minor twinges but not anything like the full assault when you experienced the familiar stimulus before changework. You have disconnected the reptilian brain's fear.

Once you access the original phobic experience, you can proceed with the normal past life healing process, clearing the event by providing an alternative reality for your persona.

Case Study: Joe had such a fear of heights that he couldn't even approach a second-story window. In regression, he went back to a lifetime when he was the designated and unwitting human sacrifice. He was incredibly terrified when the villagers dragged him up to the cliff, almost catatonic with fear as they tossed him off the cliff, and in total terror as he hurtled onto the rocks below, where his smashed and broken body suffered a quick but painful death. All of that enormous terror marked his soul.

To change that life, his Higher Self talked with the local god, who then explained to the villagers that doing human sacrifice without a willing victim was worthless, so they needed to find someone who would die willingly. The villagers immediately set Joe free.

Interestingly enough, in his newly reconstructed life, Joe came back to the village in his old age and offered to be the willing sacrifice. Although he still died the same way, this time his attitude was markedly different. His leap over the cliff was tranquil and joyous, no longer a trauma but an epiphany. By choosing that death at his time, not theirs, it resolved his acrophobia.

EXERCISE

Healing a Phobia

When you resolve a phobia, you can follow most of the steps for past life work (see Chapter 13).

1. Go back to the past life.

2. Bring in the Higher Self who will be *really* glad to help you resolve the lifetime.

3. Change the experience so it doesn't end with the same tragedy.

4. Follow the lifetime through, and watch your character die.

Your Higher Self must reclaim its lost energy for the phobia to be finally healed from its incredible psychic wound. The energy may appear as a shadow, a colored energy, as twinkles of light, etc. It must all be gathered up and returned to you.

5. Bring yourself to your inner sanctuary.

6. Call back your lost energy. Say something like, "I call all my energy back from that phobia-creating lifetime," and watch it flow into your body. Mechanisms include any of these:

   a. Become a magnet that lets your energy gravitate to you.

   b. Let your Higher Self sit in the middle of your sanctuary and breathe in the returning energy.

   c. Let the energy become heavy and fall to the ground. Gather it up and pour it into yourself through the top of your head.

7. Turn it into a cloak and wrap it around you.

8. Pick your own image.

• • •

CHAPTER 16

RESPONSIBILITY & LIFE PURPOSE

Over the last few years, more and more people have taken to blaming their parents for their messy lives: "It's not my fault that I'm the way I am," they whine. "My mother and my father screwed up my life." It's easy to blame them for the way our lives turned out; our parents did make mistakes with us—mostly unintentionally, but sometimes with malice.

Until recently, people muddled through their lives in spite of being emotional cripples, passing on to their children dysfunctions that have been in their families since Adam and Eve. By exposing behaviors once thought acceptable (drinking) or simply nonexistent (incest), we are finding encouragement to release our old dysfunctional patterns and move toward healing. One of those critically important healing processes involves blaming our abusers.

Your Inner Child knows that he or she was an innocent victim of childhood trauma. As far as they're concerned, they endured serious abuse for which they need to express rage. The blame is externalized—focused on their abusers. Releasing their pent-up rage at their parents is not only justifiable, but it is essential for the Child's healing and self-empowerment. That might mean pounding pillows in therapy, or actually suing the parent in court.

Who's Really to Blame? There's no question that your parents (and their ancestors) were at fault for perpetuating abusive behavior. You can point to many examples from your life to buttress your claim, but let's consider another answer to that question by asking why you put yourself into that abusive situation in the first place. "Me!?" you object. "I didn't choose that abuse!" In point of fact, you probably did.

Your Child was *not to blame* for her abuse. Children do not have the responsibility for adult behavior. Adults do. And your parents need to be punished for their deeds in order for your Inner Child to heal (whether that is done in changework or in the outer world). That is why you can blame your parents with impunity. They did hurt you.

But unlike your Child, *you*, as an adult, are capable of seeing your life in a larger perspective—and there is one. Your Higher Self chose your family, not only for the lessons you needed to learn, but also to resolve karma that provoked the abuse in the first place. This may be difficult to accept or believe. Who wants to acknowledge that they chose to be born into a sexually, emotionally, or physically abusive family? Nevertheless, your Higher Self didn't just choose your parents randomly; it found a family situation that would provide the best karmic lesson for you in this lifetime.

When you were a child, you had no capacity or ability to see the larger picture, but the adult can perceive, and understand, the full implications of your abuse. What you did in another life requires payback in a subsequent life.

You're not an innocent, like it or not. You've been around the block, so to speak, for many lifetimes, creating karma and paying it back, making mistakes and learning lessons from them. If your father was a sexual abuser, chances are that you did the same thing to him in another lifetime. You set up this whole experience— not to mortify yourself or provide your child with a wretched experience, but because you wanted to resolve karma. Although you don't have to like what happened to your child, it was part of your karmic lesson.

Telling your Child to accept the abuse and forgive her or his parents because of what you did in a previous life is pointless. She or he simply hasn't got the mental capacity to understand, nor the willingness. All they are aware of is the pain. Also, explaining about atonement or forgiveness merely prevents them from expressing their feelings, and creates even more anger inside them.

Responsibility

In the 1970s and 80s, the personal growth gurus proclaimed (rightly) that we were responsible for everything that happened in our lives, but they said it in such a judgmental way that made us feel wrong if we didn't face up to our situation and change it *immediately*. They didn't understand human behavior and the role shame or guilt plays in preventing us from facing our issues.

Change is a step-by-step process, most easily accomplished in a safe, loving environment, not in an accusatory or hostile one. Unfortunately, most of us tend to be highly judgmental about ourselves and others, which breeds self-guilt and blame, so that any change we undertake is painful, at best. Since you are the only one who can make changes in your life, you would most like to do it safely, in a caring atmosphere. Forcing you to look at something without preparation and little emotional support doesn't foster positive change and healing; instead it generates more trauma. It takes time, effort, and faith in your ability to make amends to face yourself and your responsibility.

Only when you're ready can you acknowledge that you might indeed have a karmic connection with the parents you chose. So now what can you do to heal the situation?

Most therapists hear clients complain, "I can't do that because my father did this to me," or "I can't succeed at that because my mother degraded me all the time." Continuing to blame your parents for your present life keeps you stuck where you are (and safe). Laying on blame like a thick blanket is easy, expedient, but not productive in the long run. It provides short-term satisfaction, but ultimately accomplishes little. However, that may be all you can handle for a long time.

Conversely, when you decide that the cause of this situation stems from your behavior in another lifetime, you can proceed to blame yourself for having done all those terrible deeds then that created this karma now. You've become a martyr. That's just as counterproductive—and equally invalid. It's important to recognize your responsibility in your past, but flagellating yourself impedes the resolution of present life issues and abuse.

In a previous chapter I mentioned Dana, who in her past lifetime had been vicious to her spouse, and was now paying the price in her present unhappy marriage. She remained stuck in that situation until she recognized her responsibility for paying off past life karma, and the necessity to terminate the abusive relationship with her husband. Once she did that, she effectively completed the karma.

You can come to terms with your present life by recognizing: 1) your abuse was karma you've *chosen* to pay off; and 2) your Child needs to be allowed to heal in appropriate ways, including expressing his or her rage at their current abusers for as long as he or she needs.

Your Inner Child knows instinctively that it is necessary to release the rage she or he carries. That is the first step toward healing the abuse. Transforming the abuse, incident by incident, starts the process of helping the Child heal. Doing changework increases your ability to release those trapped emotional toxins from both your emotional and physical bodies.

As the rage, hostility, or sadness gets expressed, it creates space inside you for perspective until you can acknowledge that you had a share in creating your karma as well. Once you've done all that, your next step is to express any other feelings that might be related to this situation. Only then can you open your heart to true forgiveness, in whatever form that takes.

Forgiveness

One New Age belief is that you must forgive everyone and everything to evolve. That's a great concept, but true forgiveness only happens after cleaning out your pent-up rage at an abuser. Many adults have told me how they forgave their parents, but when I asked their Inner Children, I found that they had no intention of forgiving the parents until their rage and fury had been expressed and transformed.

You will not burn in hell if you do not forgive your abuser, but your evolution will be harder if you don't—like a sack of boulders you're dragging behind you. You can feel self-righteous in holding on to the abuse like a precious possession: "*They* destroyed my life. Now I'm going to suffer forever. I'll show them!" Martyrdom like that gets tiresome after a while. Or "I'll make them suffer forever." It takes a lot of effort to hold on to blame, and it just perpetuates the karma.

When you are ready, you can take the next step in your healing process—forgiving the abuser. By talking about forgiving your parents (even if you reject the idea), you begin the process of reclaiming yourself from your own victimhood. Yet it cannot be done before it is time. That means you can't rush into forgiveness either. Overly eager forgiveness disregards the Inner Child's true feelings of rage, no matter how much you might like to get past them. It takes time for the Child to release those feelings, and in many cases (particularly, sexual abuse), that may not occur for a long time, maybe not even in this lifetime. Someday you will come to a point where you're ready to shift.

One reason it is so important to allow the angels to flood you with love over and over again is that it helps release that buried rage from your very cells. Once removed, *it never comes back.*

Forgiveness doesn't happen overnight; it may take years, and comes with spiritual maturity. Think of the process of forgiveness as a mortgage on your house. The first few years you're paying interest, but when you start paying off the principal (i.e., cleaning away cartloads of rage), your equity (forgiveness) starts rising precipitately. As your anger level drops, your forgiveness level rises.

You won't feel much forgiveness at first, or even for a long time. It helps if, at the end of any changework process, you ask yourself for as much forgiveness toward your abuser as you are willing to allow at this time. If you can't even ask that question, don't get upset. You've still got a lot of rage to clear away. At some point, if you ask for forgiveness, you might remove just one micron of forgiveness, but it's one micron more than you had before.

Forgiveness might not happen in this lifetime—but it must be done, sooner or later, until one day you look at your parents, your childhood, and your life, and feel love and acceptance without judgment or anger. Until that time, remember that you are working on yourself, and that's all-important.

193

Life Purpose

When you take on too much or remain in denial, or blame yourself far beyond what is right and fair for yourself, or refuse to acknowledge your part of the problem, you are out of balance. Balance comes with purpose—to assist you to stop hurting and to handle your life. Balance is a result of accepting your share of the responsibility—and no more.

In the same way, changework without a guiding purpose is aimless. Both responsibility and changework require a goal and an intent—at first, only that you stop hurting, but later on, as you clear away traumas, to manifest your life purpose. That means you must bring yourself into balance.

When you recognize that your life is not working, that is when you are more likely to reevaluate your life, and create deep, lasting change. Psychological and spiritual disciplines can clear childhood issues and mental screens, and help you become more connected to your Higher Self. Once that happens, you then are more likely to find the direction that leads to your Life Purpose.

Your Life Purpose is what your Higher Self has chosen as your task for this lifetime. Your major life task is to discover, come into alignment with, and finally manifest it. Life purposes can embrace many things; they can be in the realms of teaching, guidance, support, writing, you name it. Here are some examples: One person's life purpose involves running a ranch to preserve nature. Another's is to teach spirituality, though not intentionally from an obvious "spiritual" perspective;

yet the quality of the information has great spiritual resonance. Yet another person visits different sites around the world and energizes them with modern vibrations. These three people manifest only a minuscule fraction of all the possible life purposes.

A fulfilled life purpose enhances the quality of life of the practitioner and the people around him or her. People who gain wealth, power, or prestige by stepping on others are not manifesting a life purpose. I'm not degrading having money. It's fine to make money or wield power, but not by hurting others. Doing so is out of balance and against the divine intent.

Some people have very great life purposes—such as leading nations or the world (like Gandhi), or doing healing of some sort. It's not necessary that your life purpose fall into a particular classification (as if there were only ten possible classifications, and if you're not doing one of these ten, it is unacceptable). Your life purpose is whatever feels *right*, and that brings healing and balance to your life. It doesn't matter what your life purpose is *as long as you do it*.

Some people sense their life purpose, but their mental screens distort its message. They have an imperfect vision, which, if it affects others, can cause all sorts of damage. They say, "I have the answer, and you can get it only from me." Or they say, "I see *the truth*, and I am the only one who can preach it." Instead of guiding people to healing or new spiritual perspectives, they become destructive by limiting others, and preventing people from manifesting their own life purpose. Self-styled prophets are not in alignment with their Higher

Self or other higher beings. This type of person can include parents who decide what they want their children to be and spend their lives manipulating the children according to their own plan, which often may be counter to their children's life purpose.

The single most important purpose of changework is to clear away the baggage of the past in order for you to manifest your life purpose. When you are fulfilling your life purpose, your life is working, you are in alignment with the universe and in balance with yourself.

At first, you may not be able to understand or even conceive of your life purpose. Gradually, in doing your changework, your life purpose becomes clearer and clearer, until expressing it feels completely natural and right. You may move in several different directions to see what feels right. When you actually find that alignment, you will feel an urge to create inner change that supports and furthers your life purpose.

I have talked about being at the gold love level when you are in balance. That is a good way to describe being in alignment with your life purpose. From it, you can reach a place of love more easily, in which you feel tremendous support from the angels, and your Higher Self. You have boundless energy and love for the people around you. You know you are in exactly the right place doing the right thing.

Once you are manifesting your life purpose, you can expand and heal yourself. You are connected to your Higher Self, to the angels, to the Godhead, and in alignment with each one of your bodies.

This is the nature of your life purpose.

EXERCISE

Forgiveness

You can do this exercise over and over again until you reach a point of completion with yourself or another person.

1. Sit in a quiet spot with a piece of paper and pen. Close your eyes, clean out your aura, bring it into present time. (Don't keep parts of yourself stuck in the past during this exercise. It's intense enough as it is.)

2. Invite your Higher Self to participate with you. You'll need its help!

3. Imagine someone you want to forgive. If you do not want to see the person because the sight of him/her will get you very upset, put him/her behind a door.

4. Imagine forgiveness as a barrel of blue water.

5. Ask yourself how much forgiveness you have toward this person.

6. Even asking yourself the question may trigger enormous rage. That's perfectly fine. You have a lot of that. Imagine that rage as dark red liquid inside another barrel. (You have two barrels—forgiveness and rage.)

7. Ask your Higher Self to remove from the barrel as much rage toward that person as you are willing to release at this time. That might mean a dropper, a

197

cup, a bucket, or nothing taken out. Pour that rage onto the earth for recycling.

8. Now repeat Step 5. You might find that you are ready to express a tiny amount of forgiveness. If you don't know how much, ask your Higher Self to take out as much forgiveness as you are willing to give.

9. Pass that cup of forgiveness to the person on the other side of the door. There is no penalty for not giving out any forgiveness. As you do repeat the exercise, over time you will release more rage and send out more forgiveness.

10. Forgiveness also applies to you as well. Remove as much forgiveness toward yourself as you can accept. Many times, it is difficult for you to forgive yourself, long after your atonement is over.

11. Let the forgiveness liquid flow through you.

12. You can repeat Step 10 with your Higher Self or an angel. It's instructive to realize that other beings love and forgive you much more than you allow yourself to be loved.

•••

CHAPTER 17

HEALING
DISEASE

My friend Amy's diabetes caused the bones in her right foot to collapse, but with an orthopedic shoe she could walk on the foot without serious pain. Imagine my surprise when I learned she was in the hospital, where her doctors insisted that her foot be amputated because it was "rotting and gangrenous." She was frantically resisting their pressure, and looking for a more wholistic alternative.

Before anything could be done with her foot, we needed to find out what was happening with it that called for such a dire remedy. Amy was understandably eager to find out the cause of her foot problem and heal it non-surgically. We would start by changing the programming which had gone into the physical body.

I suggested that she ask her Higher Self to transport her back to the time when the body made the decision to lose the foot. She saw a lifetime when she was a trapper who had gotten his foot caught in a bear trap: The trap's teeth had clamped down exactly on the spot where her present-life arch had disintegrated. Although the trapper managed to free himself from the bear trap with extreme difficulty, he lost the foot in the process. The resulting wound became gangrenous, and he died.

In order for that imprinting to be removed from her own foot, Amy needed to transform that past life. In the form of a spirit, she called for help. A large, strong man showed up to rescue the trapper. He opened the trap and took the trapper to his hut to dress the wound. Although the foot bones were crunched, they did not become infected, and the trapper recovered, with a limp—Amy has a slight one now—and no loss of foot or life.

After she re-created the lifetime, I asked Amy what her foot needed to heal. She got the image of cherry bark being wrapped around the arch, across the broken bones. She envisioned herself doing that, both in the prior lifetime, and in this one. Within four days, the suppurating abscess had disappeared, and the skin was fresh and healthy. Her amazed doctors agreed that an operation was now unnecessary, and sent her home.

By releasing the body's wounding in her past life, the trauma of that wound became a memory, and the resonance that re-created the experience in this life was disrupted, obviating the loss of the foot in this present body.

Symptoms

Amy's foot is a rather dramatic example of the process of releasing illness from the physical body. When you work on the disease at its core, rather than symptomatically, you can eradicate its roots. Remember the dandelion and its taproot? Unless you remove the taproot when you chop the dandelion out, in a month or less you'll have another dandelion. Until you confront the cause of the disease, you cannot free yourself from it. You may disguise it, sublimate it, or treat the symptoms, but the cause still remains active and strong.

The physical body is intimately connected to the emotional self—as you saw with childhood issues in which the body sensation had an emotional root. Because of some weakness in a particular body area or organ, emotional pain builds up, like food heated in a pressure cooker. Unless the pain is released in some way (venting emotions, stress reduction, meditation, exercise, counseling, etc.), it increases to such an intolerable level that it manifests as a physical disorder (like a pressure cooker blowing its top).

Coronary artery blockage is a disease that is treated symptomatically, not wholistically. The treatments of choice these days are a bypass operation or a balloon angioplasty. In the first case, other arteries replace the blocked coronary arteries. In the second, a small balloon is threaded through the blocked arteries and inflated at the site of a blockage, compressing it against the wall of the artery. Although both methods work in the short term, often within a year the repaired arteries end up in the same awful shape. They get to come back for a new round of operations.

What goes wrong? Usually doctors treat symptoms, not problems. They operate on the *physical* heart without examining the *emotional* heart. Emotional pain is manifested in heart disease. Blocked heart arteries are symbolic of blocked or unexpressed love; therefore, fixing the symptom does nothing for the underlying problem.

Dr. Dean Ornish recognized that underlying issues contributed to the disease. He demanded that his heart bypass patients enroll in an intensive program that included a strict, low-fat diet, no smoking, meditation, yoga, and counseling for the patient and spouse. This regimen forced patients to confront unspoken or unexpressed feelings held within themselves, and thereby release their heart's emotional blocks, so they wouldn't remanifest as physical blocks. Though the medical establishment wanted to pooh-pooh Ornish's conclusions, they could not ignore his patients' dramatic results—little or no recurrence of the artery blockage.

Metaphor

With any disease or illness, it is important to recognize not only its symptoms, but its metaphoric significance. By seeing disease as a metaphor, you can find a reason for your having it. A good book to consult about the correspondences between disease and emotions is Louise Hay's *Heal Your Body* (Hay House, Inc., 1988). She lists all kinds of diseases, the organs affected, and the psychological meaning of each problem. If you examine the type of disease you have created, you will find you can trace its cause to your family situation, or behaviors or beliefs from your past. The originating point, however, is probably not in this life, but in another life or several.

Do you repress feelings of love or affection, or over-express love and desperate need? Are you too vulnerable to being hurt by others, or have you cut yourself off from others? Heart, chest, or lung problems indicate you have difficulty with love. Chest colds are your body's early warning about blocked or thwarted love, while heart attacks come on when the buildup of energy has become critical.

With great reluctance, the medical profession has conceded that diseases like multiple sclerosis, asthma, and juvenile-onset diabetes have a major psychological component. Although they will not admit that these diseases might have a psychological *root*, they have concluded that emotions strongly affect the progress of these diseases. Having seen too many instances where I could relate the disease or illness directly to the person's primary emotional issue, I believe all diseases have a psychological cause. By dealing with them on that level, you can effect a significant shift in the disease process.

Let's talk about the big one—cancer. Cancer cells are simply your own cells gone berserk; they are not alien invaders, like the HIV virus. Doctors can pump all kinds of toxic chemicals into the body in an attempt to kill the cancer cells, but—and it's a big *but*—they're only dealing with the symptoms, not the cause. Researchers don't know why and how you create cancer cells. Nor are they likely to find out, I believe, because they are looking for *physical* causes. In fact, cancer is a *psychological* disease—cancer cells are caused by emotional toxins that have built up in the body that finally manifest as the big C.

Here's an all-too-common example: Breast cancer is not only disfiguring, but it represents the loss of nourishment. It is related to the difficulty of many women to give and get love and nurturance easily. Women with breast cancer have issues around being loved, being able to give love unconditionally, or worthiness.

Curing cancer does not require nuking or excising the diseased organ, or poisoning the body with chemicals. It means seeking its cause and transforming it. The best tool for transforming illness into a healing life experience is through the physical body. By delving back into the past to find out when and why the body made the decision to take on the disease, you can begin to detoxify it.

Start by paying attention to where your body hurts. Common "hot spots," places in your body where you focus attention or suffer pain, include the stomach, chest, back, neck and shoulders, and head—each with its associated ailments, such as backaches, neckaches, and headaches; colds (chest or head); ulcers or other gastric or intestinal problems, including Crohn's disease, diverticulitis, or spastic colon. Destructive habits like smoking and addictions are manifestations of depression, heartache, or unhappiness, which serve to create general body degradation.

Whatever organ holds the pain has some underlying weakness that attracts toxins. It's like a weak link in a chain—the result of a buildup of toxic energies in this life and in past lives (from karma, core issues, or past life trauma to a particular body area).

Reasons for Disease

There are several reasons for taking on a disease, which directly relate to your present and past lives. When a disease develops in your body, it has a purpose and an intention, shaped by whatever lessons you have chosen to learn, and the childhood patterns you exhibit.

Here are some of the primary reasons for disease:

- To express repressed or intense emotions (which usually relate to your core issue).

- To relieve incredible emotional pressures.

- For personal emotional gain.

- Soul lessons for this lifetime.

- Karma.

- Predisposition (from past lives with the same problem).

- Core issue.

  Let's examine them in more detail.

205

To Express Repressed or Intense Emotions

By the age of three you have formed your patterns of survival. You know which behaviors will get your needs met—and which ones won't. If an emotion is deemed unacceptable (like anger) so it cannot be expressed, it remains locked in the body, where it builds up pressure (much like a stream blocked by a dam). Eventually the pressure gets so intense that the dam must burst, and it often does so, in the form of sickness or disease.

In a systemic disease (for example, auto-immune diseases like rheumatic fever, lupus, chronic fatigue syndrome, systemic cancers, etc.), the whole body participates in its collapse because the emotions connected to the initial wounding flood the whole body, reinforcing total body worthlessness. One of the most intense of those disease-causing emotions is shame. In sexual abuse, the victim not only has a strong physical reaction in and around her vaginal area, she also experiences shame over the situation, worthlessness, and lowered self-esteem—all of which flood the whole body with toxins. A physical manifestation of that emotional turmoil may be juvenile-onset diabetes, or later, multiple sclerosis.

Incredible Emotional Pressures

When pressures in all aspects of your life become so overwhelming, your body breaks down. Like the over-burdened camel whose back was broken by a little straw, your body just succumbs to the stress. For example, divorce, the loss of close relationships, or some other crisis that taps into core feelings of worthlessness, trigger outbursts or flareups of the disease process. The disease most commonly associated with stress is cancer. Generally, relentless emotional distress forces a cellular degeneration, which leads to cancer.

Stopping the disease process requires significant change—change of job, home, relationship, scenery, diet, whatever is causing the stress, coupled with positive behaviors like exercise, good nutrition, relaxation or meditation, and a radical alteration in your attitudes, behaviors, beliefs, and feelings. In this high-pressure world, cancer provides an acceptable excuse for you to make changes without appearing as though you deliberately wanted to get off the high-pressure merry-go-round. Isn't there a better way of living than trying to kill yourself?

Emotional Gain

What benefits do you derive from having a disease? Yes, having a disease has a payoff, no matter how negative it may first appear to you! How does your illness get you what you want—like attention and love? Using disease, you can create some kind of emotional well-being and self-gratification out of sickness, even though you may not realize it consciously. You may have heard it said that people get sick to get sympathy; it's their way to get emotional nurturance. In this case, the disease is generally a chronic condition, not an acute one. Emotional gain from sickness is fairly easy to spot; everyone ends up organizing their lives around the "patient." Alcoholics fall into this category.

Lessons

You come into each lifetime with certain lessons you have chosen to work on. Often a disease can give you invaluable help with issues like patience, gratitude, endurance, fortitude, and forgiveness. For a number of people, AIDS is such a lesson. Besides the issues I mentioned, you must contend with societal stigmas, judgments, and fears, as well.

Why on earth would anyone want to endure such a debilitating dying experience? There are several answers. New energies are flowing onto the earth as the Age of Aquarius takes over from the Age of Pisces. Many people are taking the opportunity to shift their consciousness, sometimes quite dramatically. AIDS has become a handy method for people to leave the planet if they so choose, or a way to work through a lot of karma in a short time.

Many people who contracted AIDS died angry and upset, while others have refused to succumb to the disease and have transformed themselves, dying with impeccable joy. (As Steven Levine has said, the act of dying can be an enormously healing experience.) Whether or not your body chooses to accept the virus (if exposed to it) and/or get full-blown AIDS is not as important as the lessons you wish to learn about yourself.

Karma

Do you wonder why some people are born with birth defects or develop illnesses such as cystic fibrosis, asthma, allergies, leukemia, or any number of genetic diseases? I believe they are expressions of karma to atone for wrongs committed in other lives. Taking on an illness and living with the emotional and physical turmoil that it creates pays off a good chunk of your debt, painful though it might be.

Predisposition

Some people have a genetic predisposition to different diseases, like breast or colon cancer, or diabetes. These predispositions merely indicate that a body weakness has built up over lifetimes, whether from uncompleted lifetimes, from core issues, or karma.

> **Case Study:** Anya had a severe problem with thrombophlebitis in her left leg. She discovered seven lives, one after another, in which her left leg was crushed, amputated, paralyzed, crippled, or rendered useless in some way. Because the original leg trauma was so intense, it left a mark on the soul that attracted more trauma to the now-weakened leg in each subsequent lifetime. Healing her illness involved healing her leg or preventing the injury from occurring in her past lives.

Taking that concept one step further, I believe that you can choose not to activate the gene for a particular disease, if you work through the issues connected to it. *That*, of course, is the kicker. You have accumulated so much "stuff" from the emotional traumas of this life and past lives, that you need to devote an enormous effort to clean them up, in order to make a shift. People end up writing books explaining how they did it; and underlying every one of those stories is a single-minded dedication to heal themselves that many of us don't have. That is what it takes—24-hour-a-day dedication, but at the end of the process, your body is remarkably free of old toxic energies.

Core Issues

Now, or in a past life, your disease is affected by, or precipitated by, your core issue. For example, if you were neglected or abandoned by a parent in one life, and your issue is abandonment, you might manifest a debilitating illness in the next to get all the attention you need (you hope). If you were imprisoned in a small place with many other people, in a later life you would want to experience a lot of space, like being an explorer. Or if you got killed in a particularly brutal way, you would want to create a safe environment.

Healing

To heal from a particular disease means disconnecting a belief system from your mind, releasing emotions associated with the problem, and resolving the causal event that keeps generating the "stuff" that keeps the disease active. This means making a serious emotional commitment to processing your feelings, regaining your lost energies, embracing your Inner Child, and changing your past life scenarios—in other words, everything I've discussed in this book.

> **Case Study:** Let's look at some disease situations. Marcy had breast cancer, and she dreaded having a mastectomy. To prevent that, she went into her

body and talked to her breasts, asking why they were becoming cancerous. The answer came back that they were unnurturing. The milk of love was not being given out. She had several children whom she alternately smothered and neglected, and a husband who was too busy with work for her. Her marriage was, in her words, "barren and lifeless," and so was her ability to give love.

I asked her to go back to the first time that she decided to create this family situation. The question led her into a past life where she was a young girl who was spurned by a man of higher station. When she married someone of her own class, she projected her bitterness at her rejection onto him and her children, so instead of giving love, she gave disdain. In this life, she lived with a husband who was unavailable to her. Along with past life and body-centered therapy for her, couples counseling helped them both work through their issues, and her breasts remained cancer-free.

Case Study: Bob was dealing with an enlarged prostate and all that that implied about his sexuality and self-worth. The diagnosis left Bob an emotional and sexual wreck. As we worked together, he recognized that his prostate problem reflected the connection between his sexual image and his self-esteem. He had used his penis as a kind of weapon within his marriage.

When he finally talked to his prostate (after much hemming and hawing), Bob learned that he had acted according to his father's beliefs about men's dominant role, repressing his own personal beliefs.

By the time he began to accept the idea that there could be other ways of acting masculine that were not nearly so destructive to him, the prostate stopped growing, with no further development after several years without treatment.

These examples illustrate how nothing exists in a vacuum; a problem with one self creates a resonance throughout the others because they all are interconnected and interdependent; therefore, treating the five selves as a group, not individually, promotes full body healing.

EXERCISES

Healing the Disease

There are a number of exercises in this book that can be applied and adapted for healing a disease. The childhood exercise (Chapter 8) and past life exercise (Chapter 13) are particularly useful to heal the emotional self and the soul. Auric cleanout in phobias (Chapter 16) will remove disease energy. Finally, you can adapt the mind exercise in Chapter 6 or use the second exercise below on beliefs. Don't forget the reversal exercise in Chapter 7, since reversal is very common in disease.

1. Lie comfortably, eyes closed. Soft music helps.

2. Invite your Higher Self to come with you to talk to your disease.

3. Imagine going down an elevator or escalator to the focal point of the disease. For a systemic disease,

ask your body to provide a spokesperson to explain the disease's purpose.

4. Ask for your body's purpose in manifesting the illness. You may receive pictures, sounds, feelings or sensations. You *will* get some kind of message. (If you don't perceive anything, your mind doesn't want you to hear the message. It has an investment in keeping the status quo, no matter how destructive for the whole being.) Be persistent. Ask your Higher Self to help, if necessary. Your body *does* want to tell you what's wrong. After all, it's in pain and it would like the pain to stop, preferably without its death or maiming.

5. If you get a past life image, use the past life procedure in Chapter 13.

6. If the body part appears angry at you (you can tell), ask what it needs from you—whether it's acknowledgement, atonement, an apology, or commiseration. You'll be surprised at how often the organ in question will be more than delighted at getting an apology. Mainly, *it wants acknowledgment* more than anything else for enduring all the stress of your life situation.

7. Ask your body whether it wants to be cured. *This is very important.* Part of your healing may actually mean suffering from this illness (this is a karmic issue).

8. To release karma, call on an angel.

   a. Ask it how much karma it will forgive—some or all of it.

b. Then ask that the angel remove the karma from your diseased organ. You can picture it as a color.

9. Now ask your body, your Higher Self or an angel, what the body needs to heal. Perhaps it means doing Inner Child work (Chapter 8), past life work (Chapter 13), or forgiveness (Chapter 16). Or just accepting what your guides and angels tell you.

10. Ask your organ what kind of a gift it would like to make it feel happier. A rainbow, an individual color, a gem, a song, all of these may be acceptable—also a vacation, a new diet, change in lifestyle, etc.

11. Ask your Higher Self and the organ for any remedies it might need which might be applied on the inner level or in actuality. (Amy didn't have cherry bark on hand, but she visualized it on her foot.) The body might say, "I need a hug," or "Soak me in water," or "Take me away from here!" It will *not* say, "Cut me off," unless that leads to a greater good, like saving your life (and even in that case, it would have to be pretty serious).

12. Clean out the area.

a. Flood the area with a color. Green is an all-purpose healing color, but blue, gold, or violet will do.

b. Breathe the sound "*aum*" into the area. This vibration helps break down emotional blockages.

c. Put your hands on the area if you can get to it, or have friends do so, and breathe fresh energy and healing into that place.

13. Visualize the area sparkling clean and healed.

14. Forgive yourself for hurting your organ, however unconsciously. Part of the work of forgiveness is letting yourself experience joy. It's much easier to flagellate yourself into sinlessness than enjoy yourself.

15. Thank your organ for being willing to talk to you.

16. When you finish the process, do not assume that everything has been resolved. You have layers and layers to get rid of. Keep on recalling your healing visualization (step 12). If you don't see anything, just use your feeling. Make it as strong as possible.

Releasing the Belief

You will be looking at the belief attached to the disease and disrupting it. (Much of this exercise is similar to the exercise on pages 76–77.)

1. Go into your sacred room, and invite your Higher Self to join you.

2. Find your magic mirror on the wall and ask it to show you the body part that is hurting, in images, feelings, or words.

3. Ask that organ what belief is associated with its sickness. Often you will experience a feeling like shame or guilt or fear. Attached to that emotion, you may have a belief, often, "I'm worthless," "I'm unlovable," "I'm no good."

4. Enhance that feeling so it fills your body, however uncomfortable it makes you. The more of it you feel, the more you will get rid of.

5. Imagine a large sunken bathtub filled with gold liquid. Climb into it. Sink all the way down so the liquid covers your head (you can breathe in gold). Imagine the gold liquid dissolving away the emotion you are feeling. A good image is of rock salt dissolving in water.

6. Say affirmations that counter that belief embedded in your organ. "I'm worthless" becomes "I'm worthwhile." "I'm not lovable" becomes "I'm lovable." "I'm no good" becomes "I'm good." This way you can recalibrate your belief system at the cellular level.

7. Repeat the following affirmations. As you do, imagine the words being absorbed into the diseased part like silver glitter. This transforms the belief.

   a. "I love myself. I love [name the affected organ]."

   b. "I forgive myself. I forgive [name the affected organ]."

8. If more emotion comes up, repeat steps 4, 5, and 6.

• • •

CHAPTER 18

HEALING THE PAST

When I decided to write this book, I imagined it as a healing process for me, as well as a manual that others might find useful. At the time, I wanted to focus on the psychological issues, but as the book evolved, I realized that I was expressing part of my own spiritual journey through my writing.

I have long recognized that we have chosen to come to this planet for a larger purpose than to scramble to survive year after year. We have come here to fulfill our life purpose, whatever that may be, which may be specific to this lifetime or part of a much larger pattern that extends through many lifetimes. Yet underlying this life purpose is something even more profound—the self-evolution of a soul, and the evolution of humanity, in its many forms.

We all left the Godhead on our great journey of learning, innocent as newborn babies. With the first decision we made, we lost our innocence, never to be reclaimed—but that has not been the purpose of our journey. If it were, we would have remained attached to the Godhead, as angels. During this long, long period of existence, we have made wonderful connections, incredible mistakes, joyful creations, great blunders—all necessary elements of any evolutionary process.

We chose that arduous and tortuous route toward transcendence, toward wisdom, toward reintegration with the Godhead, in a far more wonderful way. Innocence is charming but limiting; wisdom creates total harmony with the will of the Godhead, tempered with the experience of self and the manifestation of life purpose.

This is the journey I have undertaken, along with many others. Some of us recognized that they have been on this path forever, while others are just now awakening to the call of self-transformation. Many of us feel that we are fighting to transform while drowning in a sea of unwanted and yet uncontrolled patterns, needs, emotions, and fears that have attached themselves to us from our earliest childhoods. How can we overcome them on our way to the manifestation of our life purpose and self-evolution? I felt an enormous frustration at being trapped in those old patterns and fears. I wanted to break away and become a new person—and yet, I was scared of what I would become.

I began with a desire to put the past to rest, to get rid of the attitudes, patterns, and behaviors that had haunted me like the luggage from hell for most of my life. I thought that meant going back to my childhood and making inner changes that would release those patterns, but I found that that was only part of the process.

I needed to transmute those feelings, needs, and fears into something positive that could help me evolve. I imagined it, not like only dropping the battered luggage, but giving it to someone who wanted whatever I was willing to get rid of. Or if it was no longer useful, allowing it to be recycled—with my blessing and good wishes.

I like to call it "evolving." It means focusing not on the past but on the future—moving toward a goal, however amorphous it might appear at the present, that defines and expresses my life purpose.

I can guarantee you that our life purpose is *not* to be regurgitating our childhood until doomsday. Healing from our childhood *is* a necessary step in order to move toward fulfilling our life purpose, but not the major one. By being stuck there, we lose sight of our own inner divinity, our own inner wisdom, and our chosen path. I'm saying all this, not from a perspective of lofty detachment, but because I have spent a long time in the trenches of childhood pain and unhappiness.

Finally, I realized that we cannot evolve unless we stop floundering around in our childhood, call a halt to all that inner angst, and begin to direct ourselves and our lives toward a new vision—the vision of what we want to be, rather than where we have been.

The most important thing I learned was that staying stuck in the past made it difficult for me to create a healing, loving, or wise present or future. I was limiting myself because of my childhood fears, old patterns, and my desire to not change (it was safer being the way I had been). Besides, all the work on childhood hadn't made an enormous dent in my basic behavior.

When I started my work, I didn't have any idea about life purposes. I only knew that what I was doing wasn't working for me, and I let my Higher Self guide me. I continued my work as a psychic; I found that chunks and pieces of my confusion disappeared until I gradually found myself seeing a clearer picture of my life and its purpose.

Because of that, I began to guide other people into their own inner world to release their blocks and fears. Since I wanted to be sure my work was safe and impeccable, that I wasn't going to create another kind of wounding, I became a transpersonal psychotherapist, working to bridge the spiritual with the psychological. The results have been quite positive and healing for my clients—and myself.

I still found that many of my clients, and I, myself, used the excuse that childhood was the source of all our problems, that nothing short of a lobotomy was going to break through the dysfunctional patterns forged during that time. Perhaps it is still so, but I have reached a place now where I don't feel quite so pessimistic, or at least, I'm not willing any longer to be controlled by my past.

That's the purpose of writing this book, to give you tools and techniques that will help you release the tyranny of the past in its many forms, and let you embrace your life purpose, whatever that is.

The question you might ask after reading this book is "Can you do any of this yourself?" and the answer is "Nobody else can." You could have a friend read the steps, or put them on tape and stop the tape and process, but the fact is that only you can do what needs to be done. It takes only willingness and openness to healing.

The process is ongoing and multilayered. It's like a spiral. Once you work on an issue and think you've cleared it, it recurs later on, maybe in a different form but with the same old intensity—coming from a deeper level from this life, and from a past life. That's why the process is so relentless and interminable. We're doing double duty—not only do we work to heal this life, but all the earlier lives as well. The process takes time (read "forever"), and yet we do create significant change. That's the only constant in our lives.

We chose to be here on this planet, at this time in history, not because we wanted to leave, but because we wanted to resolve karma—for ourselves, our family groups, the country, and the planet. We wanted to do it now, so that at the end of this lifetime, those of us who are ready can choose to move on to the next level of evolution.

It can only be done once we have come to terms with being here, once we have let go of all of our old restrictive baggage. We *can* do it—if we remember that we are not doing this alone; we are in partnership with our Higher Self, the Godhead, angels, and with whomever we want to bring in to help us. It is a joint effort—it does not need to be drudgery.

One of the most important things to remember is that with each process, you are supporting your self—the creation, breaking free of the limiting behaviors, beliefs, needs, and negative emotions that have run your life so far. That means you will find yourself making different choices about your lifestyle, your friends, family, work situations—all based on your life purpose, rather than inner emotional needs. Transformation is creating the possibility for unlimited expansion of being.

I've addressed the problems you might encounter as you are transforming yourself, but I haven't mentioned what you will transform yourself into. I don't know what you will be like when you are completely changed. Personally, I think you will be a wonderful, magnetic being of light.

What I do imagine you will be, as you keep transforming, is more aware psychically and spiritually of yourself and others. There is much I haven't said about spiritual transformation and awareness; that is beyond the scope of this book.

The hallmark of spiritual awakening is the boundless urge for transformation, whether it manifests as simply the desire for change, or a restlessness to step beyond ourselves. Eventually, it comes down to healing our dysfunctions and pains, and moving into lightness of being—what has been called "walking lightly on the earth." That doesn't mean we have to lose weight; it means that our bodies (our five selves) become lighter in energy because they are no longer filled with blocks, alien energies, or stuck in places that dragged us down. We appear normal, but inside we are filled with joy—perhaps not every day of our lives, but for a considerable number of them.

Many people have written of the spiritual journey. All I can add is that I envision, for those of us who choose to step forward into that transformation, a fuller awareness of, and connection to, all living things, not only humans, but animals, plants, and the planet itself. Then we will be in balance and in harmony with ourselves, and expressing our highest good. I look forward to every one of us attaining that level.

•••

REFERENCES

Callahan, Roger. *Why Do I Eat When I'm Not Hungry?* New York: Avon Books, 1993.

Chopra, Deepak. *Ageless Body, Timeless Mind.* New York: Crown Publishers.

Dickinson, Alexandra. *Following Your Path.* Los Angeles: Tarcher Books, 1991.

Gawain, Shakti. *Creative Visualization.* San Rafael, CA: Whatever Press, 1978.

_____. *Living in the Light.* San Rafael, CA: New World Library, 1986. All of Gawain's visualization books are excellent.

Hay, Louise. *You Can Heal Your Life.* Santa Monica, CA: Hay House, Inc., 1987.

_____. *Love Your Body.* Santa Monica, CA: Hay House, Inc., 1988.

Levine, Steven. *Who Dies?* New York: Doubleday, 1982.

Ramer, Andrew & Wylie, Daniel. *Ask Your Angels.* New York: Ballantine, 1994.

Redfield, James. *The Celestine Prophecy.* New York: Warner Books, 1992.

Roberts, Jane. *The Education of Oversoul Seven.* New York: Prentice Hall, 1984. Any of Roberts' "Seth" books is mind-expanding. This one was particularly good for seeing the world in a completely different way.

Roman, Sanaya. *Living With Joy: Keys to Personal Power & Spiritual Transformation.* Tiburon, CA: HJ Kramer, Inc., 1986. Or any of her other books. Very good for visualization and spiritual transformation.

Stone, Hal, and Sidra Winkelman. *Embracing Our Selves: The Voice Dialogue Method.* San Rafael, CA: New World Library, 1989.

Taylor, Catherine. *Inner Child Workbook.* Los Angeles: Tarcher Books, 1990.

Weiss, Brian. *Many Lives, Many Masters.* New York: Ballantine Books, 1988.

_____. *Through Time Into Healing.* New York: Ballantine Books.

Stay in Touch. . .

Llewellyn publishes hundreds of books on your favorite subjects. On the following pages you will find listed some books now available on related subjects. Your local bookstore stocks most of these and will stock new Llewellyn titles as they become available. We urge your patronage.

Order by Phone

Call toll-free within the U.S. and Canada, 1–800–THE MOON.
In Minnesota call (612) 291–1970.
We accept Visa, MasterCard, and American Express.

Order by Mail

Send the full price of your order (MN residents add 7% sales tax) in U.S. funds to:

Llewellyn Worldwide
P.O. Box 64383, Dept. K601–7
St. Paul, MN 55164–0383, U.S.A.

Postage and Handling

- $4.00 for orders $15.00 and under
- $5.00 for orders over $15.00
- No charge for orders over $100.00

We ship UPS in the continental United States. We cannot ship to P.O. boxes. Orders shipped to Alaska, Hawaii, Canada, Mexico, and Puerto Rico will be sent first-class mail.

International orders: Airmail—add freight equal to price of each book to the total price of order, plus $5.00 for each non-book item (audiotapes, etc.). Surface mail—Add $1.00 per item. Allow 4–6 weeks delivery on all orders. Postage and handling rates subject to change.

Group Discounts

We offer a 20% quantity discount to group leaders or agents. You must order a minimum of 5 copies of the same book to get our special quantity price.

Free Catalog

Get a free copy of our color catalog, *New Worlds of Mind and Spirit*. Subscribe for just $10.00 in the United States and Canada ($20.00 overseas, first-class mail). Many bookstores carry *New Worlds*. Ask for it.